—— THE ULTIMATE ——
SITUATIONAL
SURVIVAL GUIDE

SELF-RELIANCE STRATEGIES
FOR A DANGEROUS WORLD

ROBERT RICHARDSON

IR

Living Ready BOOKS
IOLA, WISCONSIN
www.LivingReadyOnline.com

CONTENTS

PART FOUR:
Surviving Man-Made Disasters, Threats, and Terrorism

PART FIVE:
Surviving Financial and Economic Threats

Introduction

Help isn't coming!

It may sound harsh, but the reality of most crisis situations is that you're going to have to be your own first responder. When disaster hits, or when confronted with an unexpected threat, there's a very good chance you're going to have to survive on your own with only the knowledge and training you possess. With that in mind, how prepared are you to survive a real-life crisis situation, or deal with the chaos that will ensue during the aftermath of a catastrophe?

- Do you have a detailed plan in place to deal with disasters or crisis situations?
- How long could you last without essential services like water, power and sanitation?
- Do you know what the most likely threats are to your safety based on your geographic location or lifestyle?

The main purpose of this book is to motivate you to take action. To motivate you to put the right plans in place to see you through a crisis and ensure your ability to protect yourself and your family from a wide range of very real threats and disasters. By implementing the plans and strategies in this book, you will be able to survive everything from short-term natural disasters to long-term economic problems, breakdowns in society and social unrest, and infrastructure failures or disasters.

This is not another Wilderness Survival Manual; this book is your guide to surviving real-life 21st century threats. These are the threats you are likely to face—the kind of threats you need to start preparing for if you want to survive.

What are you willing to do to guarantee your survival? What are you willing to do to guarantee your family's survival?

Hopefully you are willing to do whatever it takes. That being said, you need to have a plan of action. This book will lay the groundwork for that plan and will help you build a rock solid preparedness foundation. I'm not going to lie to you—it will take some work on your part. But I believe you owe it to yourself and those you love to take a serious look at the concepts detailed in this book.

PART ONE:
Situational Awareness:
Prepare to Survive

Despite what you may have seen on so-called "Reality" TV survival shows, preparedness is more than just guns, gear, and bunkers full of food. Survival has nothing to do with some guy running through the wilderness performing a bunch of stupid stunts. Living through actual disasters, dealing with real-life threats, and protecting yourself from the dangers that are out there requires you to adopt a survival mindset and to develop your situational awareness.

In this section I will help you

- identify what threats are out there, and help you spot them before they can do you harm.
- manage your exposure to threats, access your vulnerability, and help you do everything possible to completely avoid a catastrophe.
- lay out a detailed step-by-step plan for surviving crisis situations, including actions to take for surving during the aftermath.

① Know Your Threats

Do you know what you're preparing for? It may sound like an odd question, but most people really don't have a clue.

To begin with, you need to understand the exact types of disasters and threats you're going to face. This may sound a little simplistic, but not all disasters are created equal. What works in one situation, or in one area of the world, may not work when you factor in specific location-based threats.

While some of the supplies, techniques, and skills you need to survive may overlap, to be truly prepared for any situation you need to know exactly what type of disasters you're preparing for and what problems you'll most likely encounter as a result of that specific disaster.

In later chapters I will discuss how to identify and prepare for disaster-specific problems. But to get the most out of this book, and to be prepared for the specific threats that will most likely affect you, you're going to have to do a little work.

That work starts with identifying the most likely threats you'll face based on your geographical location, your lifestyle, and a number of other factors that will be unique to your specific situation. The following section will help you get started with your preparedness planning.

THREAT ASSESSMENT

A threat assessment helps you visualize what threats you'll face, scrutinize known risks related to the threat, strategically evaluate your response, and helps you start to identify the specific steps you need to take to stay safe. It's going to help you protect the people you love from harm.

There are three primary objectives when performing a threat assessment:
1. Identify the threat.
2. Assess what needs to be protected.
3. Manage your exposure to the threat.

When performing your threat assessment, keep the following things in mind:
- Who/what needs to be protected when disaster strikes?
- Who/what are the most likely threats you will face based on historical data?
- What can be done to minimize your exposure to each of the threats?
- What are your vulnerabilities and how can you manage or get rid of them?

STEP 1: IDENTIFY THE THREAT

The first step in analyzing your overall preparedness is to identify the most likely threats you'll face based on where you live, your lifestyle, and historical trends.

What Are the Most Likely Threats You Will Face?

Make a realistic list of what the most likely threats are and how the threats will affect you should you face them. This should be a location-specific list; if you live in the Mojave Desert, hurricanes probably shouldn't be on the list. That being said, when traveling to a new area on vacation, I always do a mini threat assessment before leaving.

Identify Scenario-Related Threats

Under each threat, make a list of your vulnerabilities based on that specific threat. What problems do you foresee happening when the threat strikes? Think about disaster-specific threats as well as threats that may come from how people react to the disaster.

Identify Personal Threats

Do you or anyone in your family have any personal considerations that could be exacerbated due to each of the identified threats? These can include medical conditions, age-related limitations, mobility issues,or specific dietary needs that might be hard to meet during a disaster.

Identify Aftermath Threats

After the initial threat has passed, are there any threats you expect to spring up as a result of the disaster? These can include power outages, looting, home invasions, or anything that may be specific to your location. For instance, if you live near a nuclear reactor that could be affected by the initial disaster, this would definitely be a threat you need to list. Consider what happened as a result of the Japanese earthquake/tsunami that crippled Japan's Fukushima Daiichi nuclear reactors.

IDENTIFYING THREATS TO YOUR NEIGHBORHOOD

Location-based threats may not be immediately apparent, but I bet there're more potential threats in your neighborhood than you've probably considered.

- Is there anything about your town that makes you a likely terrorist threat? This can be anything from a large population base to military bases or chemical plants that can be easily targeted.
- Do you know what types of chemicals local businesses use in their production processes? Industrial accidents can have devastating effects on neighboring communities.
- Do you live in a flood zone or an area that's at higher risk for a specific type of natural disaster?
- Do you know about local crime patterns or have any idea of how many local gangs are in your area?

The first step in minimizing your threat to a hazard is awareness. You need to take a serious look at your immediate area and figure out what potential dangers exist.

Railways and Highways

Deadly chemicals, flammable and explosive substances, and even radioactive materials are shipped daily on the nation's highways and railways. Most chemical accidents are caused by transportation accidents. Even people living in the most remote areas of the country cannot completely insulate themselves from danger. In fact, if you live anywhere near a highway or a railway, there's a pretty good chance you have hazardous chemicals traveling through your area on a daily basis.

Chemical Plants and Industrial Buildings

It's estimated that in the United States alone, some 4.5 million facilities either store or use hazardous chemicals and materials. Many of these facilities are allowed to operate in or near residential areas, where a hazardous material accident or chemical spill could quickly overtake a neighborhood.

From obvious places like industrial plants and chemical waste sites to not-so-obvious places like hospitals, dry cleaners, and food processing plants, you need to be aware that hazardous material accidents can happen anywhere.

Most communities have Local Emergency Planning Committees that are responsible for knowing what chemicals are being used in a community and developing plans to deal with emergencies involving those chemicals. Your local Emergency Planning Committee should be able to provide you with this information and is the first place I would start. These committees are usually run by local government officials and/or local fire or law enforcement departments.

Find out what chemicals are being used near your home, and find out what plans and warning systems are in place.

Hazardous Dams and Levees

Besides being an obvious terrorist target, almost one-third of U.S. dams are over fifty years old, the average lifespan of most dams. Even more troubling is the fact that somewhere around fourteen thousand dams are classified as high-hazard, meaning that any operational mistake could cause a significant loss in human life; two thousand are so bad that they have been rated structurally deficient, meaning they are at a high risk of failure.

Most Americans are unaware of the problems and don't even realize their homes lie directly in the path of an inundation zone. Because the government restricts most maps from showing inundation zones, check with your state's dam safety agency or talk to local emergency management officials about potential dangers.

Crime, Gangs, and Criminal Organizations
According to the FBI, there are over 1.4 million active gang members and around thirty-three thousand different gangs in the United States. What was once largely an urban problem has now spread into even the most rural areas of the country.

COMMON THREATS THAT FOLLOW ANY DISASTER
While the aftermath of each disaster will be specific to the situation, there are some general repercussions that play out during almost every type of disaster.

Economic Problems
Depending on the severity of the disaster, there's a good chance you could take a major economic hit. From not being able to access your bank accounts due to power outages caused by a natural disaster to longer-term problems like the inability to work due to illness or workplace closures, consider the possibility of lost income.

- How prepared are you for the economic aftermath of a disaster?
- Do you have enough cash on hand to make it through an extended period of time in which you might lose access to your bank accounts?
- Do you have a way to supplement your income if a disaster hits your workplace? What would you do if your company suddenly closed down or you were laid off?
- Do you have enough food, water, and emergency supplies on hand to survive the possibility of not being able to buy more?

Essential Services Shutdown
During almost every type of local or regional natural disaster, you are probably going to face at least a few disruptions in essential services. Electrical grid and

energy failures, water shortages and shutdowns, and the disruption of telecommunications routinely happen during even small-scale disasters. Losing these essential services means losing the ability to

- heat or cool your home.
- light your home using regular light fixtures.
- keep food fresh through refrigeration or freezing.
- cook inside your home.
- communicate with the outside world and gather information.
- stay clean and healthy.

To be ready for essential services shutdowns

- you must be prepared to survive without gas and electricity for an extended period of time (at least two weeks).
- you must be ready for financial service shutdowns, specifically the inability to make electronic payments during a disaster.
- you need to have backup water and sanitation systems in place in case of water emergencies or sewage system shutdowns.

Breakdown in Food Distribution and Delivery Systems

Food, water and emergency supplies are going to be incredibly difficult, if not impossible, to come by following a disaster. During disasters that cause major road closures and breakdowns in fuel distribution, you may have to live off the supplies you have in your home for an extended period of time.

Supplies are hard to come by leading up to and following a disaster for two reasons: a breakdown in delivery systems and panic buying from people who failed to prepare.

- If disaster struck right at this moment, how long could you last with only the supplies you have in your home?
- If fuel shortages dried up gasoline supplies, do you have enough gas in your tank to make it out of town?
- If delivery systems were disrupted, do you have enough medical supplies to make it through an extended disaster?

Potentially Lethal Sanitation Issues

When planning to survive any long-term disaster, something that's often over-looked is the danger associated with a lack of adequate sanitation. I know it's not a pleasant thing to think about, but if faced with a situation where sewage systems stopped working and garbage trucks stopped running, sanitation is-sues could quickly become a life-threatening problem.

Breakdown in Social Order

In the aftermath of a major natural disaster or economic collapse, violence, looting, and an increase in criminal behavior is almost a certainty. Unfortunately, the world is filled with people who love to take advantage of these types of di-sasters for their own personal gain. To be truly prepared, you need to be able to defend yourself during the aftermath of any type of disaster.

STEP 2: ASSESS WHAT NEEDS TO BE PROTECTED

The next step in the threat assessment process is to assess how each of the identified threats will affect you and then figure out what needs to be done to protect yourself and your family from those threats.

- How will each of the threats that you identified affect you, your family, your property, and your current survival plans?
- Based on the identified threats, do you see any vulnerabilities that need to be addressed ahead of time?
- What supplies do you need to stockpile to help survive the threats? In-clude things like food, water, protection, shelter, medical supplies, and anything you've identified under the personal threats section.
- Are there any areas in your plan, security, or overall preparedness efforts that need to be addressed? What steps can you take right now that will help protect yourself, your family and your property from danger?

STEP 3: MANAGE YOUR EXPOSURE TO THE THREATS

The final step in the threat assessment process is to take immediate protective actions that will help prevent or minimize your exposure to the identified threats.

- Start to outline an emergency response plan and a threat reduction strategy for each of the listed threats.
- Take the time to research each individual threat. Are there past events that affected your area that you can learn from? What did people do during these previous disasters that might help your situation? Knowledge is the key to survival; the more you know about the threat, the better chance you have of surviving it.
- Address and fix any of the vulnerabilities that you identified during the threat assessment.

PROTECTING YOURSELF FROM THREATS TO YOUR NEIGHBORHOOD

Most of the location-based threats you'll face have dedicated chapters in this book that contain detailed survival strategies. In addition to those strategies, keep the following in mind.

You Need an Evacuation Plan

Many localized emergencies can be survived simply by leaving the area, so having an evacuation plan is vital to your safety. In the case of something like a chemical spill or terrorist attack, where seconds can literally mean the difference between life and death, you need to have multiple routes out of town.

You Need a Bug Out Bag

Because time is of the essence during any evacuation, you can't afford to waste it on packing up emergency supplies. That's why it's so important to put together a bag of emergency supplies, called a bug out bag, that can be grabbed at a moment's notice.

Always Have Cash on Hand

If you need to quickly evacuate, having emergency cash can help you do everything from rent a hotel room to stock up on extra supplies. Remember, you can't count on being able to use electronic payments during a crisis situation.

EMERGENCY PREPAREDNESS SWOT ANALYSIS

Now that you've performed a realistic threat assessment, the next step in the preparedness process is finding out how prepared you are to face each of the identified threats. To do this, you need to perform something called a SWOT (Strengths, Weaknesses, Opportunities, Threats) analysis.

A SWOT analysis is a simple but useful method of really understanding

- Strengths that can be helpful during a survival situation.
- Weaknesses that can make survival a challenge.
- Opportunities that you can exploit to your advantage.
- Threats that you might face during an actual survival situation.

Performing a SWOT analysis on yourself, your family, and your capabilities is a great way to determine how prepared you are to face the unique challenges of surviving any crisis.

STRENGTHS

When identifying your survival strengths, a good place to start is to take an inventory of supplies you currently have. This can be everything from food and ammo to knowledge or specific skills you might possess.

Analyzing your strengths will give you a good idea of what you're capable of doing. It's also a great way to highlight and use overlooked things that could be extremely beneficial during a survival situation.

- What survival gear, equipment, and tools do you currently own? Really think about this one because it can include regular items in your home that might be of use during a disaster (blankets, first aid kits, outdoor grills, lanterns, existing food stockpiles, tools, etc.)
- Do you have any skills or training that might be useful during a survival situation? These can be handyman skills, CPR training, communication training, or anything that may be useful during a crisis.
- What resources do you have in your area that can be exploited during a survival situation? Are there local sources for finding wild food or emergency water?

- What do you consider your best personal traits? Make a list of what you feel are your general everyday strengths, and then determine if these strengths will be useful when disaster strikes. Consider attributes such as confidence, good decision-making skills, adaptability, and even positivity. During a survival situation, it's often these types of skills that ultimately determine the outcome of the situation.

WEAKNESSES

This is where you really have to be honest with yourself. Honestly detailing your weaknesses will help you better prepare to survive a crisis situation. When you know what your weaknesses are, you can take steps to deal with them so they don't hinder you in a crisis.

- What skills do you lack or need to improve?
- Do you have any emergency supply or gear deficiencies that need to be addressed?
- Is there anything about your location that could be considered a weakness (lack of natural resources, security vulnerabilities, high crime rate, aging infrastructure, etc.)?
- Do you have any medical problems or personal issues that could become a liability during a disaster? Do you have a plan to deal with them?

OPPORTUNITIES

Try to imagine what resources and opportunities are available to you and what will be around when a disaster strikes. List the opportunities you can take advantage of as well as those that will be important during a survival situation.

- What resources and opportunities can you exploit in your area when a disaster strikes?
- Are there any opportunities you can take advantage of that will help strengthen some of your weaknesses (local classes, survival courses, the library, websites, or any other learning resources)?
- Do you have a network of people you can rely on during a disaster?

THREATS

To truly be prepared, you need to have a realistic idea of what threats are out there and how likely it is that each of those threats could happen. By going through this exercise, you can better prepare yourself to face any scenario a disaster may throw at you. You will know exactly what skills you need to work on, what plans you need to put in place, and what equipment you will need.

This should expand on your threat assessment and take into account any secondary threats that could result from the initial disaster.

- What added obstacles will you face based on the threats in your threat assessment?
- What are the immediate dangers in your location (aging infrastructure, nuclear plants, chemical plants, lack of resources, etc.)?
- Who is the biggest threat in your neighborhood (gangs, criminals, unprepared neighbors, etc.)?
- Take another look at your weaknesses. Can any of them seriously threaten your survival?

THE NEXT STEP

The most important part of performing a SWOT analysis is what you do with your findings. There's no point in performing one if you don't plan on taking action. Now that you have a good idea of the disasters you could face and your overall level of preparedness, you need to act on your findings and create a strategic plan of action. The next chapter will help you create that plan.

Develop Your Personal Action Plan

"If you fail to plan, you are planning to fail."—Benjamin Franklin.

When it comes to surviving a disaster, the single most important thing you can do is have a plan. Planning helps take the stress out of the situation and allows you to tackle it with a clear and focused mind, which is vitally important to your survival.

Survival situations can create unimaginable amounts of stress, severely compromising your ability to think clearly and take decisive actions. Creating a well-thought-out plan before the crisis hits can often be the determining factor in your ability to survive that situation.

When formulating an action plan, consider everything you worked on in the threat assessment and SWOT assessment exercises in chapter one. If you skipped over anything that was suggested, you might as well put this book down and hand your survival over to fate. I can't understate the pre-planning process—your life could depend on it.

In order to formulate a plan that works, go through each and every step, fully understanding exactly what you're planning for, and then putting contingency plans in place based on everything you identified in your SWOT analysis.

Here are five key things to keep in mind during the planning process:

1. How long can you survive without essential services (power, water, gas, and the ability to purchase food)? What do you need to do to meet each service need on your own?
2. What tools and supplies are needed to survive the threats outlined?
3. After disaster strikes, what steps need to be taken to survive?

4. What things will determine whether you stay and hunker down or pack up and get the hell out of Dodge?
5. If you have to evacuate, where will you go, how will you communicate, and what is needed to survive an extended period away from home?

Carefully examine your threat assessment and SWOT analysis and think about the previous five points. After you have a good grasp on everything, it's time to formulate a plan of action to face whatever threats might come at you. When it comes to emergency planning, I'm a big proponent of putting everything in writing. Not only will it help you remember your procedures during a time of crisis, but it will also help you find any weaknesses or overlooked vulnerabilities you may need to plan for. During a disaster, your plan can help put your mind at ease and can help you avoid making bad decisions when your mind may be clouded by fear.

After you have your plans in place, you need to practice and make sure everyone in your group or family is on board.

THERE'S NO ONE-SIZE-FITS-ALL PLAN

When it comes to survival, far too many people are looking for the easy way out. In an attempt to shortcut the process, that easy way out usually involves buying a bunch of prepackaged garbage that's being marketed as the solution to survive any disaster. There's no such thing as a one-size-fits-all solution to all your survival and preparedness needs. If you believe that nonsense, I've got a bridge to sell you...

The Fallacy of the 72-Hour Survival Kit

A 72-hour survival kit is a collection of emergency supplies that are meant to help you make it safely through a natural disaster. While this may sound like a good thing, I believe the 72-hour time frame sets people up to fail. It gives a false sense of security and grossly underestimates the amount of emergency supplies you'll need to survive most disasters.

The 72-hour number was first conceived, and is often used, by government officials who estimated it would take government aid agencies at least 72 hours to reach survivors during a disaster. While the government may want to use that as a baseline number, recent disasters suggest 72 hours is really not the number you should be preparing for. For instance, when Hurricane Sandy hit New Jersey in 2012, residents were left without power and essential services for weeks, in some cases months. While the 72-hour kit may have helped them for a couple days, it did little to prepare them for the actual hardships they had to face in the aftermath of the disaster.

Unfortunately, unscrupulous marketers have run with the 72-hour time frame and used it as a gimmick to sell crappy supplies to unsuspecting people. If you see one of these prepackaged survival kits being sold at your local store, do not even consider buying one. Most of the time, these prepackaged bags are complete garbage. They're usually filled with items that nobody would ever need or use during an urban survival situation. They contain, for example, things like flimsy wire saws that are totally unusable in an urban or even wilderness setting.

When it comes to preparedness, there is no-one-size-fits-all plan for survival. That's especially true when it comes to buying survival gear. Everyone has unique survival needs that depend on a wide variety of factors.

If you're serious about preparing yourself and your family for disaster, I suggest building your own emergency stockpile, with the thought process of having to survive for a minimum of two weeks. Later in the book, I'll discuss why I think you need a three-to-six month stockpile of food and water, but for the purpose of surviving your typical natural disaster, I think two weeks is a pretty good start.

Two weeks' worth of food, water, and emergency supplies should give you more than enough wiggle room and will see you through most natural disasters. It gives you ample time to either get things back to normal or make alternative plans that may include the need to temporarily evacuate.

WHAT SUPPLIES DO YOU NEED TO SURVIVE A DISASTER?

This is probably one of the most common questions I receive; in fact, I probably receive at least a couple e-mails every day from people asking for gear recommendations. Survival gear is a highly debated topic on survival blogs, websites, and online forums, but the focus on specific gear sometimes overshadows what's really important: Your survival gear is only as good as your knowledge, planning, and training.

Newbies, and even some old-timers, often obsess over their gear. Sometimes they put so much emphasis on their gear that it can actually become detrimental to their ability to survive. Many people live under the delusion that they're prepared to survive anything life has to throw at them because they have loaded up on survival gear. But that's not how life works, and it's definitely not how survival works.

If you lack the necessary survival skills or fail to properly plan, all the fancy gear in the world isn't going to save you during a disaster. If I had to choose, I would take my training, knowledge, and skills over any piece of fancy survival gear, any day of the week.

That being said, I do love my gear as much as the next guy, and provided you've put in the work—completing your threat assessment and SWOT analysis, starting your emergency preparedness plan, and training and learning necessary survival skills—the right equipment makes surviving a disaster a whole lot easier.

After you have a good grasp on what's needed to survive, start choosing the survival gear and emergency supplies you need to buy. If you're just getting started, focus on the basics first:

- water
- food
- shelter
- protection
- first aid, medical concerns, and sanitation

These are the fundamental building blocks to any good survival stockpile and should be the foundation on which you start.

YOUR SURVIVAL SUPPLIES ARE UNIQUE TO YOUR SPECIFIC NEEDS

While most books will give you detailed lists of the top 101 survival items that will "help you make it through any disaster," this one will not. In my opinion, most

The survival gear you choose will be based on a number of factors. Your location, your skill set, and the most likely disasters you'll face all need to be taken into consideration before choosing any piece of gear.

of these lists are worthless. While they can help give you a general idea of the type of items you might need, there is no one-size-fits-all survival plan. Telling you to stock up on beans and rice when someone in your family might have an allergy to those items really doesn't do you much good, does it?

Instead of giving you a list of items that may or may not be useful to you, I will give you some guidelines that will give you a good place to start. If you take the foundation that I lay out—water, food, shelter, medical items, and protection—and start to expand on it based on your unique needs, you will be prepared to face almost everything a disaster can throw at you.

Here are some considerations you need to keep in mind when putting together an emergency supply stockpile.

- **Start with what you know.** Based on your threat assessment and SWOT analysis, list the items you believe you'll need to survive each individual threat.
- **Role play the threat.** Try cutting the power in your home for a week, or even a day as a place to start. Experience is the best teacher you can have and is the only way to determine what you actually need. Based on your experience, what things did you need to survive? Were there certain items you were lacking, and on the other side of the coin, was there anything you could do without?
- **Plan on being without basic services for an extended period of time.** Electricity, gas, water, telephones, and even sewage treatment could be cut off for days, weeks, and in some cases much longer. Do you have a plan to survive without each of those services? What items can you stock up on that will make it easier on yourself and your family?

- **Don't underestimate the importance of entertainment and comfort.** A large part of survival is mental. After you lose the will to survive, all the preparation, gear, and planning in the world doesn't really matter. When building your survival stockpiles, remember to include comfort foods and a way to entertain yourself and your family during the disaster (board games, cards, etc.) If you have kids, this step is critically important to their well-being and should not be overlooked.

EMERGENCY PLANS FOR YOUR PRIMARY SHELTER

If at all possible, taking shelter at your primary residence is usually the safest option following most natural or man-made disasters. Most of your supplies are probably going to be at your home, and in most cases you will have a higher level of security inside your home than you will traveling on the streets.

While sheltering inside your home is often the safest bet, there are some considerations to keep in mind.

You Must Always Be Prepared to Leave.

No matter how badly you want to stay, there will be times and situations that make it impossible. If a Category 5 hurricane is barreling toward your location, the last thing you want to do is shelter in place.

Home Security Needs to Be a Top Priority.

The ability to defend your home from those who wish to do you harm is one of the most important considerations you need to prepare for. Home security is a top priority during any disaster.

Neighbors May Come Knocking.

During a disaster situation, your not-so-prepared neighbors are going to be in panic mode. While most of these people might not pose an immediate threat, if things get bad enough, those once peaceful neighbors will become unpredictable. You must have a plan in place to deal with those who failed to prepare.

TRAINING WITH SURVIVAL ROLE-PLAYING

I believe training and preparation are so important to your survival that if you skip over everything else in the book, I hope you at least do this one exercise. The amount of knowledge you'll gain by doing this exercise is worth the hassle and the stress it's inevitably going to cause.

You will be far better off making mistakes and dealing with a little bit of stress during a training exercise than making those same mistakes when it counts—when you can't flip the power back on to save yourself from a bad situation.

To really do this right, you need to pretend you're living through an actual natural disaster, and you need to do it for at least a couple of days, preferably a whole week. Your family should be on board with the plan, but they probably shouldn't know exactly when it will happen. The surprise element is important because during most natural disasters you're probably not going to have a whole lot of warning. Pick a date and flip the switch. For an entire week, act as if you are in the middle of an actual disaster.

- Go to your electrical panel and cut the power to your home. And no cheating on this one, unless it's an emergency! I'm pretty sure the kids will live without the T.V. for a week; they might even come out better on the other end. One caveat I should mention is making sure you don't lose any of the food in your refrigerator or freezer. If you don't have a generator, consider leaving the power to those appliances on.
- Cut the water, and stop using anything that requires an outside utility. With this one, I will allow you a little bit of wiggle room. Before cutting the water, fill up as many containers as you can find. That, and anything you have stockpiled, should be your primary

source of water for the week. (If you run out, remember this is a training exercise, not some stupid reality show where you put your family through hell, seeing how long they'll last. Just make a note in your journal that water is something you need to work on, refill your water containers, and continue with the exercise.)

- Have clear and specific goals and objectives that you want to get out of the exercise. Keep detailed notes on how you performed, what you need to work on, and what things you did right.
- Have fun with it, and make sure everyone is involved in the process. This is especially important if you have children, and will give you an entirely different perspective on the situation. You may even learn something from them.

Ask children questions throughout the process:

- Find out how they feel things are going.
- Ask them what they would do during certain situations.
- Ask them what they would do differently and how they feel about the plans you have in place.
- Find out what they think is important to make it through a real-life situation. Keep in mind that with kids, a lot of their answers may revolve around comfort and entertainment, which is extremely important to their mental well-being during a time of crisis.

If you do this one thing, you will probably learn more about your level of preparedness than anything else you could ever do. Just remember to keep detailed notes and act on your findings. Going through the process means nothing if you don't act and improve on what you learned.

GET HOME BAGS

Having a get home bag is an essential element of any well-rounded get home plan. Unlike a bug out bag (discussed in chapter five), which is meant to help you survive an immediate evacuation, a get home bag's sole purpose is helping you get back to your house if you are away when a disaster or emergency strikes.

What goes in your bag is largely a personal decision that should be dictated by your own unique circumstances. In general, it should be a lightweight bag that's filled with only the items you need to survive the trip home. Keep in mind that depending on the disaster and how far you are from home, you could be walking for quite some time, so pack accordingly. Here are a few things you might want to think about carrying:

- Water. This also includes a canteen and way to purify water if you plan on being more than a 12-hour walk from home. (Iodine tablets are easy, lightweight purification options.) I prefer canteens or water bottles made from high-grade steel for their ability to boil water right in the container.

Be Aware of Urban Areas

If you live in a high-density population center, you immediately put yourself in danger and make your chances of survival lower than if you lived in a rural area. While I'm not saying sheltering in place won't work in an urban setting, it will become increasingly harder as the severity of the disaster increases.

GET HOME PLANNING

When planning for any type of disaster, one of the most overlooked areas of concern is what happens during the immediate aftermath of the disaster. Even

- Emergency food, preferably high-protein, high-energy foods like nuts, trail mix, and energy bars
- Walking shoes
- Sunglasses and a hat
- Emergency clothing (specific to the season)
- Protection: firearm and a knife
- Communication gear, emergency cell phone, and handheld ham radio with backup batteries
- Extra cash. This could come in very handy during certain situations and should not be overlooked. Remember electronic payment systems will likely be down, so you need to have some paper currency on you at all times.

Check the contents of your Get Home Bags at least once every three months to restock it with seasonally appropriate gear and replace any expired contents.

more problematic is what happens when you find yourself away from home when disaster strikes.

Since a majority of us spend so much time away from our homes, having a get home plan is essential to your survival and your ability to make it home during a natural disaster.

Identify Multiple Ways to Get Home

For most people, their workplace is where they spend the majority of their time away from home. So odds are good that if you're not home when a disaster strikes, you probably will be at work. So it's extremely important to have multiple routes mapped out that you can use during a disaster to get you back to your home. Your emergency routes should include indirect routes, back roads, and even walking trails, as major highways will probably be blocked or highly congested during any emergency situation.

These resources can help you identify routes:

- **Printed road maps.** I suggest investing in a good local road map, as well as maps of your surrounding area and a national atlas. These should be kept inside your vehicle at all times, and should be filled with notations on what routes you plan on taking.

- **Google Maps.** A great way to be better prepared is to map out your get home routes with Google Maps. With the aid of their satellite view, you'll find up-to-date detailed routes that might not be listed on normal maps. It also gives you the ability to plan out multiple alternative routes, including walking routes and backcountry trails. Mark these routes on your printed road maps, or print them out and keep them inside a binder in your vehicle.

- **Electronic maps.** While I would never rely on anything electronic as my primary means of navigation, advances in navigational technology make it impossible to ignore the benefit of using GPS and smartphone/tablet technology. To get the most out of these devices, store offline versions of maps on them and carry an external power source (e.g., hand-crank or solar charger) so you can use the device when off the grid.

Communicate While Getting Home

If at all possible, one of the first things you should do during an emergency where you are going to be walking or traveling through a sketchy environment is to communicate your plan to loved ones. A short call, text, or e-mail letting them know that you're putting your get-home plan into action will give them peace of mind and ensure they don't needlessly put themselves in danger looking for you. See chapter four for details on emergency communication planning.

EVERYDAY CARRY KITS

Let's face it, having a 30-lb. (14 kg) bag full of gear at your side at all times is pretty impractical. Yes, you can have multiple bags stashed at your home, office and even in your vehicle, but no matter how much you prepare there will be times when you become separated from your gear. That's why I suggest always having an Everyday Carry (EDC) kit.

Every Day Carry kits or EDCs are an essential part of being prepared. I think everyone should get in the habit of carrying one of these kits.

What Is an EDC Kit?

An EDC kit is made up of items you should have on your person at all times. In most cases, your EDC kit should be small enough to fit in a pocket and it should only include gear and supplies that are absolutely necessary to help you survive in an emergency situation where you basically have only the clothes on your back. An EDC kit will help get you to your main source of supplies, or provide you with enough supplies to make it through the emergency at hand, making it an essential part of any good survival plan.

As with all survival gear, your EDC kit needs to be customized to meet your specific location and survival needs. Items that you should always carry as part of your EDC include

- cell phone
- handgun (with concealed carry permit)
- cash
- multitool with knife
- survival kit

The Infamous Altoids Survival Kit

I always carry a small metal candy tin (think Altoids tin) filled with survival supplies that would be useful in a survival situation. Because I often travel in remote areas, my kit is filled with items suited for that setting. Likewise your kit should be filled with items that fit your unique needs and location. If you live in an urban area, most of the supplies I carry will probably be useless to you, so keep that in mind when choosing what gear you pack.

My Altoids kit includes (and remember it's geared for a wilderness setting, so adjust to meet your needs)

- pocket knife (Swiss Army style)
- basic medical supplies (butterfly bandages, tweezers, scalpel blades, and small magnifying glass that can also be used for starting fires)
- spool of dental floss (multiuse: cordage, fishing line, medical uses such as suturing wounds)
- tinder (cotton shoved into all the little crevices)
- a couple of needles, fishing hooks, and fishing weights
- disposable cigarette lighter and a couple of matchsticks cut in half with a striker in plastic wrap
- small LED flashlight
- bandana wrapped around the case

Knife Sheath EDC Kit

In addition to my candy tin EDC, I also always carry a knife sheath kit. This kit allows me to carry a decent size knife while still being able to carry a number of items in the front pocket of the sheath.

In my knife sheath kit, I carry

- SOG SEAL Pup knife
- disposable cigarette lighter wrapped with duct tape and fishing line (in between the line and the tape there are a couple of needles and a single fishing hook)
- SOG multitool
- mini LED flashlight
- 550 Paracord wrapper

Stockpiling Survival Supplies

As I mentioned in chapter two, there are five foundational categories that are the building blocks to any good survival stockpile:

- water
- food
- shelter
- protection
- first aid, sanitation, and medical concerns

With this foundation in place, you set yourself and your family up to survive almost any type of disaster. This chapter details how to create stockpiles for each category.

WATER

In a survival situation, water is going to be one of your top priorities. Simply put, if you don't have it, or you can't find it, consider yourself as good as dead.

How Much Water Do You Need to Stockpile?

The average person who engages in a normal amount of activity typically drinks about two quarts (½ gallon, or 2 liters) of water every day. Although this number may be a good place to start, it doesn't account for additional factors including environmental conditions, medical conditions, and even sudden illness that can strike during a disaster. Because a crisis situation is usually filled with so many unknown variables, I advise bumping that figure up to at least a gallon of water per person, per day with the mindset that you'll probably be without access to fresh running water for a minimum of two weeks.

How to Store Your Water

Buy bottled water. The safest and most reliable method of water storage is to purchase commercially packaged bottled water. This water is already packaged for long-term storage and is a good way to start your emergency water supply.

Fill food-grade water containers. When it comes to storing water, I recommend only using food-grade water storage containers. These containers can be found anywhere, from surplus and camping supply stores to the camping aisle at your local discount department store.

Refill empty beverage containers. If you decide to use your own containers, make sure they're made from high-quality food-grade material. Two-liter plastic soft drink bottles are going to be your best option, as they are already made to store liquids for a long period of time. Stay away from milk and juice bottles as these types of containers are almost impossible to completely clean and can become a breeding ground for bacteria.

Water Storage Safety

If you decide to bottle your own water for storage, sanitize the containers you will use with a liquid bleach solution. This solution can be made by adding 1 teaspoon of liquid chlorine bleach to a quart of water. Shake the solution in the bottle, making sure it touches every surface, and then thoroughly rinse with clean water.

If you're filling your containers with commercially treated water from a public water utility, there's probably no need to add anything to the water as it's already been treated with chlorine.

If you're using water from another source, such as well water, add ⅛ of a teaspoon (or 8 drops) of unscented liquid household chlorine bleach per gallon to maintain water quality while in storage.

Storage Time

Unless you're storing commericially bottled water, it's a good idea to replace your stored water every six months. Your water should be stored in a cool, dark area with the fill date or purchase date written on the outside of the conatainer.

URBAN WATER SOURCES

Your home has a number of places where you can find emergency water in a pinch:

- **Hot water heater tank.** Your hot water heater has a drain valve where you can obtain the water from the tank. Read your water heater's manual for detailed instructions.
- **Canned goods.** Tuna, canned vegetables, beans, and fruit all contain liquids that can be drained out and used as a source of hydration. Unlike the other water sources listed here, this water does not need to be treated before you drink it.
- **Drain your pipes.** If you live in a multilevel home, you can drain the water in your pipes by using gravity to your advantage. After the water lines into your house have been shut off, drain your pipes by using the lowest faucet in your house.
- **Toilet water.** In an emergency, you can boil the water from the flush tank (not the bowl) of your toilet. I would only use this water as a last resort and only if I was sure it was free of cleaning chemicals.
- **Rainwater.** Use large pots and containers to catch and store rainwater.
- **A note about pools.** While this water is not drinkable because of the high amount of chlorine in it, it can be used for bathing and washing dishes or clothes, which is important during a survival situation.

In the case of store-bought water, observe the expiration date on the bottle. That being said, most water wil keep indefinitely.

How to Make Water Safe to Drink

Even the best emergency plan needs a Plan B. When it comes to water storage, this means knowing how to find and sanitize water during an emergency.

While there are a number of options for cleaning contaminated water, none of them is 100 percent effective at treating everything. The best methods for killing bacteria and other microorganisms include boiling, chemical treatments, and water filtration systems. For detailed information on water purification and dealing with water emergencies, see chapter twenty-nine.

FOOD

While food isn't as vital as water (you can survive a long time without eating), it is an important consideration. Having a full belly can greatly help morale and your mental state during an emergency. With the rising cost of everything, food is becoming a significant part of every family's budget. In fact, it's estimated that the average American family spends over 12 percent of its budget on food. With that in mind, the thought of spending even more money to stockpile an emergency food supply might seem a little overwhelming for some.

While the extra cost might seem like a burden, the fact is, we all need to have a stockpile of emergency food on hand at all times. This stockpile can save you both during a natural disaster and during a job loss.

Stockpiling on a Budget

Stocking up on emergency food doesn't have to break the bank, and you don't have to buy commercial survival food to "be prepared." Here are some ways to save:

Look for foods that have a long shelf life. Things like hard grains, most flours, beans, pastas, and canned foods are all excellent examples of foods that will last.

Don't buy foods that you don't eat on a daily basis. There's no use buying a bunch of food that's going to just sit on a shelf. Your emergency food supply should be primarily made up of foods you already eat, so they can be rotated into your existing food supply and used up without going to waste.

Stock up around the holidays. Holidays are a good time to score some great deals on canned goods. If you have an extra freezer, you can stock up on things like turkeys and hams at a fraction of what they'll cost at other times of the year. If a natural disaster cuts your power, cook your refrigerated and frozen food first before it goes bad and then start using your shelf-stable foods.

Buy when it's on sale, and become an extreme couponer. You don't have to spend hours upon hours clipping coupons, but you should take advantage of every chance you get to save money. Most major food manufacturers offer money-saving coupons through their websites, local newspapers, social media pages, or other online resources. Make these coupons go even further by using them during double or triple coupon offers.

Types of Food to Stockpile

The two best principles for selecting food for your stockpile are

1. Make sure you think it tastes good.
2. Make sure you eat it on a regular basis.

When people first start stockpiling food, they usually make the mistake of stocking up on foods that they would never eat in a non-survival situation. Buying that twenty-pound bag of beans might be cheap, but an emergency situation is not the time to start trying foods that may disagree with your body.

Stock up on foods that you normally eat on a day-to-day basis. Now I don't mean stocking up on things that can spoil, but you should definitely stock up on foods that your family is familiar with and enjoys eating.

Don't forget comfort foods. Maintaining a positive mental attitude during a stressful situation is an extremely important aspect of survival. Don't discount the need for stocking up on foods that will help you pick up your spirits during tough times. Sweets can provide both a quick calorie boost and a morale boost in an emergency, especially for children.

Flavor, flavor, flavor. Stock up on flavor enhancers like salt, sugar, honey, and shelf-stable spices that store well. Again, comfort and familiarity are an important part of survival.

Regularly Rotate Your Food Stockpile

Don't forget to rotate your stocks. Rotating your emergency food supply into your regular diet is smart for a couple of reasons:

- Using a first-in, first-out system of rotation will guarantee that your food is as fresh as possible. You'll also cut down on waste by using up food before it has spoiled or expired.
- It ensures that your body will be able to handle the food that you intend to survive on during an emergency. If you're eating it now, chances are you will want to eat it during a disaster.
- It gives you a good idea of how much food you have on hand and where any shortfalls might be.

SHELTER

Your ability to regulate your internal body temperature and protect yourself from the elements is extremely important during any type of survival situation. Shelter is a survival necessity that can literally mean the difference between life and death. The type of shelter you choose will depend on your situation, environment, and overall ability to improvise shelter from local materials.

Many natural or man-made disasters can shut off vital utility services, meaning you may not be able to heat or cool your home as usual. This is why shelter remains an important consideration even if you plan to stay in your home.

Some items that you should consider include

- extra blankets and quilts, sleeping bags, winter clothing, hats, and winter coats
- space blankets and chemical hand/body warmers
- extra firewood for your fireplace
- portable space heaters, propane heaters, or kerosene heaters
- portable tents and plastic sheeting (this can be used to block off a section of your home to create a warm zone, which will be much easier to heat than trying to regulate the entire home's temperature)

During an emergency, a small room or closet can easily be turned into an insulated fortress. Couch cushions, blankets, towels, and mattresses can be used to add insulation to your warm zone area. You can also line your clothing with crumbled-up newspapers, paper towels, or any other insulating materials.

FIRST AID, SANITATION, AND MEDICAL CONCERNS

During most natural or man-made disasters, sanitation can quickly become a huge problem. From losing the ability to access safe water and waste facilities to outbreaks of mold and disease that can often happen during the aftermath of a disaster, you need to have a plan in place that addresses your sanitation needs and medical concerns.

Keeping clean is the first step in keeping healthy. Here are some tips for how to stay clean even if water and sanitation services are unavailable.

- Keeping your hands clean during an emergency is the first step in preventing the spread of disease. If your tap water becomes unsafe, create a temporary hand-washing station using a jug filled with water that has been boiled or disinfected.
- Use only disinfected, drinkable water to brush your teeth. Bottled water is best, but the water from your hand-washing station can also be used provided water services in the area haven't been compromised by a storm related-chemical spill.
- You need a plan to deal with waste. That means garbage and human waste. For the purposes of preparedness, a simple five-gallon (19-liter) bucket can work well in a disaster situation. If you lose water pressure, water can be poured into the flush tank allowing you to still flush the toilet. If all else fails that bucket can be filled with a plastic bag, some sand or dirt, and topped with a toilet seat. After each use, add another layer of sand or, better yet, cat litter.

It's important to have a good first aid kit stocked with items you can use to disinfect, clean, and cover wounds. If anyone in your home has a medical condition, your first aid kit needs to be stocked with extra supplies and medications that will see that person through the disaster.

PROTECTION

Disasters can bring out the worst in people. Despite what some politicians would like the public to believe, firearms save lives. I'm not going to recommend any one firearm; you're going to have to figure that one out on your own. Just like with other areas of preparedness, there is no one-size-fits-all gun for every situation, and what works for me might be totally wrong for you.

I advise going to your local gun store, where you can try out a variety of guns until you find one you're comfortable with. Then you need to seek out a qualified instructor who can teach you how to use that firearm in a real-world self-defense situation.

Firearm Basics: Gun Safety

Firearms owners bear a responsibility that needs to be taken seriously; it's literally a matter of life and death. Since every gun is different, before handling any firearm you need to thoroughly familiarize yourself with it. Even if you consider yourself an expert, before handling any new firearm, you need to understand the particular characteristics of that gun.

All too often, I see gun owners who let their ego get in the way of good common sense safety practices. These are guys who have been shooting for years, but are too proud—or too stupid—to ask for help.

I can't tell you how many times I've seen someone at the range take an unfamiliar firearm from a friend, without ever asking a single question about that firearm. *Never assume you know the gun.*

Before you accept a firearm someone is handing you, proper gun safety requires you to

- **Ask if it's unloaded.** You should always ask if the firearm is unloaded before taking it from anyone. If the person answers yes without checking, ask them to show you.
- **Check for yourself.** It's your responsibility to check for yourself; don't ever take someone's word! Point the muzzle in a safe direction, and if the firearm has a safety make sure it's on. Immediately check to see if the gun is loaded. Just because your friend told you it was unloaded

doesn't mean it is. Always treat every firearm as a loaded weapon. There is no such thing as an unloaded gun.

- **Ask for help.** Don't be the person who was too proud, or too stupid, to ask for help; that person is a danger to himself and everyone around him. When taking an unfamiliar firearm, you should always ask the person handing you the firearm to show you the particular characteristics of that gun. Every gun is different, from the location of the safety to how it handles. Never assume you know how it works.

When it comes to handling a firearm, there are some basic rules that should always be followed.

1. **Always point the muzzle in a safe direction.** If people followed this one rule, virtually all firearm accidents would be eliminated. Remember, your firearm should never be pointed at anything you don't intend to shoot.

2. **Never rely on your gun's safety.** While your safety should always be on when you're not shooting, it should never be counted on to prevent the gun from firing. A safety is a mechanical device that can and will fail; it should never be 100 percent relied on to stop an accident.

3. **Keep your finger off the trigger.** If you're not in the process of firing your firearm, your finger should not be inside the trigger guard. The Internet is loaded with pictures of idiots posing with their finger on the trigger. This practice is not only stupid, it's likely to get someone killed.

4. **Practice, practice, practice.** If you can't remember the last time you fired your gun, you're doing yourself and your family a disservice, and you're putting your lives at risk. To be a good and safe marksman, you need to practice your shooting skills. Practice not only makes you a better shooter, it also ensures your firearm is in good working order when you need it. The last thing you want to find during a self-defense situation is you have a gun that's not in a condition to be fired.

5. **Make sure you are using the right ammo.** Using the wrong type of ammunition can seriously damage your gun and can cause serious injury to yourself and those around you. Although this seems like common

sense, it's actually a common mistake that even some seasoned hunters have made out in the field. For example, a common hunting mistake is to accidentally load a 20-gauge shell into a 12-gauge shotgun. This can be a deadly mistake that can cause the barrel of your shotgun to blow out when the lodged shell creates an obstruction inside the barrel.

6. **Know where you are firing and what's beyond your target.** After you pull that trigger, you can never get that shot back. Unless you know exactly what you're shooting at, and what lies beyond what you're shooting, you should never take the shot. Even a small round like a .22lr bullet can travel a distance of about 1¼ miles (two kilometers); this means you better be darn sure of what's beyond your intended target.

7. **There's no such thing as an unloaded gun.** Drill that saying into your head because it's probably the most important safety advice you'll ever receive. Every firearm you touch should be considered a loaded weapon; therefore, it needs to be given the respect due a loaded gun.

Emergency Communication

During any type of crisis situation, establishing communication is going to be one of your top priorities. Unfortunately, despite huge advancements in communication technology, our modern infrastructure has left us incredibly vulnerable to disaster-related communication outages.

From cell towers being overwhelmed by a flood of traffic during the initial stages of a disaster to entire sections of communications infrastructure being shut down because of power outages, even a small-scale disaster can wreak havoc and limit your ability to communicate.

Let's face it—most of us are always on the go, and since we can't predict exactly when and where a disaster will strike, there's probably a pretty good chance you may not be with your family during the onset of the crisis. Because of the unpredictable nature of disasters, you need to have a plan that guarantees you'll be able to find your loved ones during an emergency situation. That means developing an emergency communication plan and making sure everyone in your family knows what it is and how to put it in place during a disaster.

YOUR EMERGENCY COMMUNICATION PLAN
Step 1: Make an Emergency Contact List
Start with making a list of your emergency contacts. This list needs to have the most up-to-date phone numbers, e-mail addresses, and even your contacts' social media accounts. If there's a way to get in contact with them, it should be on the list. Provide this information to everyone in your family or survival group.

If you have young children, this information should be printed out on a index card that they can keep with them at all times. They will have a difficult time remembering information like this during times of crisis, so it's vital that you provide them something that can jog their memory.

Step 2: Designate a Point of Contact
Your emergency contact list needs a central point of contact. This should be a close friend or family member, preferably one who lives out of state and will not be affected by localized disasters, who can coordinate emergency planning efforts until everyone finds their way back together or to safety.

Your designated contact person also needs to have an up-to-date copy of your emergency contact list and should immediately inform everyone on the list of the specific details of the situation. This ensures that if something happens to the designated contact, or should someone not be able to make contact, everyone on your list will be on the same page and can help coordinate communication efforts. The designated contact should start a group e-mail, or some sort of status update system where people can easily check the status of the situation without clogging up phone lines. Social media can be a great way for family members who are not in immediate danger to receive these status updates.

Step 3: Establish a Last Resort Rally Point
Should all other methods of communication fail, your family should have an emergency rally point where everyone meets up during a disaster. This point should be outside of your immediate area and needs to be somewhere that can be easily found and reached by everyone in the group.

PUTTING YOUR EMERGENCY COMMUNICATION PLAN INTO ACTION
After a disaster strikes and you have removed yourself from harm's way, one of your first priorities should be putting your emergency communication plan into action.

1. **Immediately call your main point of contact.** This should be one of the first calls you make. The call should be short, sweet, and to the point. What's important here is giving a quick status update, including who you've heard from and what your plans are so everyone in your

group or family is on the same page. During this call, establish a set time that you plan on checking back in.

2. **Emergency status e-mails and texts.** If possible, try to shoot out a group text and/or a group e-mail to everyone on your emergency contact list. Let them know you're OK and that your main point of contact is coordinating things. It's a lot quicker than calling everyone and has a better chance of getting through on cell networks that will likely be congested during an emergency.

3. **Social Networks.** If you're not in immediate danger, post a quick update to your social networks. This can help give people in your family peace of mind, and can inform everyone of your plans and how they can find you. It's also a great way to share status updates that will keep the phone lines open to those who really need them.

EMERGENCY COMMUNICATION GEAR

During a disaster, it's very likely that most communication channels will go down. Hopefully this will only be temporary, but either way you need to plan for the worst-case scenario and have multiple options available to you.

Cell Phones

I'll start with cell phones because these days almost everyone has one. While cell networks are often overwhelmed during the initial phase of any disaster, they still might be useful if you know what to do.

If your initial attempts to make a call fail, try texting or using your phone's data plan to make contact with everyone on your list. As we've seen during past disasters, texting and even social media apps can sometimes work, even when voice calls don't. A text message takes a lot less bandwidth than a phone call, so during a disaster this might be your best bet for making contact.

Social Networks

While you'll still need a device and Web service to access them, social networks can be a great way to communicate during a disaster. If you can make your way to an emergency crisis center or access them on your cellphone, you might be able to post a status update to your social networks.

While I wouldn't rely on this as my primary means of communication, it can be a great way to let friends and family know you're safe, or let them know what you're planning on doing next. During a disaster you need to have as many options as possible.

Satellite Phones

While satellite phones are on the expensive side, during a natural disaster or crisis, having one just might save your life. Satellite phones offer a couple of advantages during a disaster. First, they don't rely on local cell networks, so they're less likely to be affected by an increase in call volume. Second, even if the entire local cell network goes down, your satellite phone is still going to be operational. This makes them a definite plus if you can afford one.

CB Radios

I know, you're probably picturing big-rig trucks or bad movies from the 1980s, but the fact is, a CB radio can be an important part of your emergency communications arsenal. I recommend having one in your vehicle, carrying a handheld radio in your bug out bag, and having a base station at home.

During a localized disaster, you should be able to use a CB radio to make contact within a twenty- to thirty mile-radius (thirty-two- to forty-eight kilometers). This makes a CB radio a great way to coordinate with friends and family during localized disasters.

FRS/GMRS Two-Way Radios

The Family Radio Service (FRS) and the General Mobile Radio Service (GMRS) are designed for short-distance, two-way communication. They're generally used with small walkie-talkie devices and have a range of somewhere between five to thirty-five miles (eight to fifty-six kilometers) and about one mile (two kilometers) in an urban setting. While the range might be a problem, they can be useful in caravan situations where you're traveling in multiple vehicles with a group.

Ham Radios

Owning and knowing how to use a ham radio is probably one of the most important things you can do to ensure your ability to communicate during a disaster.
For over a hundred years, the ham radio has played a vital role in almost every
major disaster.

When the grid goes down, the cell networks stop working, and every other
line of communication fails, there's a pretty good chance the ham bands are
going to be alive and operating. Just remember to have a set list of frequencies
where you and your group will try to make contact.

Bugging Out: Planning to Evacuate

While riding out a disaster in your home should be your first plan, when everything goes downhill, there are times when your only option may be to bug out. To ignore the fact that an evacuation may someday be inevitable is not only shortsighted, I think it's a major hole in any survival plan. To truly be prepared, you must consider the possibility of having to evacuate from your home.

GOVERNMENT-ISSUED EVACUATIONS

If you waited for your local government to issue an evacuation notice, it's probably too late. The last thing you want in any emergency situation is to get caught up in the chaos of the crowd. Mindless morons will be everywhere, and mandatory evacuations almost never go well.

The highway system simply is not set up to handle the overwhelming influx of traffic caused by a mandatory evacuation order. Time and time again we see highways overwhelmed, so much so, that even during small-scale natural disasters it's not uncommon to see people sitting in traffic for hours—only to have moved a couple of miles from their starting point.

DECIDING TO "GET THE HELL OUT OF DODGE"

Deciding when to go is an important part of your evacuation planning process and needs to be thought of now, not when you're in the middle of a full-blown crisis situation. This one decision is probably the most crucial part of your plan and needs to be thoroughly thought through.

Identify what factors and threats will determine when and if you should leave your location. Write these down as part of your plan. For example, if you live in an area prone to wildfires, you may decide you will bug out when fires are sighted within a mile-specific radius of your home. Identify key cities or landmarks at the edge of that radius and as soon as you hear of fire reaching there, start your bug out plan.

In any evacuation, timing is everything. You must be able to recognize the signs of an impending disaster, and then have a plan in place to deal with it.

PLANNING TIPS FOR EVACUATIONS

Don't Ever Rely on GPS

During an evacuation-causing disaster, the last thing you want to do is rely on your GPS. Doing so sets you up for disaster, as you will likely be funneled into a choke-point with tens of thousands of evacuees who are all following the same GPS routes.

Have Multiple Routes Out

Now is the time to plan your evacuation routes, and part of any good evacuation plan is to have multiple routes out of the area. During times of crisis, the road-ways are going to quickly become congested. Depending on the situation, they may become impassable, either due to weather or government-issued road-blocks. Having multiple preplanned evacuation routes will ensure your safety and can help put you hours ahead of the mobs of unprepared evacuees.

- Consider what you will do if your routes become blocked or impassable.
- Think about alternative routes you may need to take that are off of your main escape route.
- Make sure you consider food and water options along your routes. Knowing where you can stop or refill your supplies is important.

Look at Alternative Routes

If things get bad enough, you may have to get off the roads. That means you have to take into account alternative routes, which include off-road trails, service routes, and even hiking and mountain biking trails. I recommend plotting these routes out ahead of time using a tool like Google Maps.

A Bug Out Location Is Crucial

Leaving without a place to go is not a plan. If you plan on bugging out, you need to have a predetermined bug out location or emergency shelter already in place. Planning on living in the wild, unless you are an extremely experienced outdoorsman, is a recipe for disaster. Wilderness living should only be considered if you have an adequate shelter already in place, and even then you are taking some serious chances with your life. Every good evacuation plan includes a list of locations where you would go during a disaster. The last thing you want to do is put yourself at the mercy of some government-run evacuation center. As we saw during Hurricane Katrina, you might be better off taking your chances on the street.

Your evacuation plan should include the following evacuation locations:

- **A meeting place directly outside your home.** Earthquakes, fires, or disasters that directly affect the safety of your home require a meeting spot just outside your home. This should be an area close to your home, but not so close that you put yourself at danger from the threat.
- **A friend or family member's home.** The next emergency evacuation point should be a close friend or family member who is outside the danger zone. This should be a place you can easily get to during localized disasters.
- **An out-of-state friend or family member's home.** For disasters that affect an entire region, you need to have a place you can head that puts you far away from harm. If you have family members or friends who live out of state, talk to them ahead of time about using their home as an evacuation point.
- **Hotels or RV parks.** If you don't have access to a friend or family member's home outside your area, take the time to put together a list of hotels or RV parks you can head to during an emergency. They should be far enough outside your area that they won't be overrun by other people fleeing the same disaster.
- **Dedicated bug out location.** If you have the financial means, your best option is going to be having a dedicated emergency shelter filled with everything you need to survive an extended emergency.

A DESIGNATED BUG OUT PROPERTY

When it comes to buying a bug out location, location is the key. Here are some of the top considerations that you need to keep in mind when looking for the ultimate bug out property.

Distance

If you're purchasing a piece of property to serve as a bug out location, you need to consider how far that property is from your current home.

- How far is the retreat from your current location, and are you able to safely make it there during a crisis?
- Can you make it to your bug out property on a single tank of gas, and if not do you have a plan in place to find enough gas to get you there during an emergency when gas may be hard to come by?
- How far is the property from high-density population areas? I believe the farther you can get away from people, the safer you will be.

Water Sources

A good reliable water source is one of the most important considerations when choosing a bug out retreat. From freshwater springs and rivers to underground well water, the need for a clean and renewable water source is one of the top factors when looking for bug out properties.

- What water sources are on the land?
- Are they renewable and will they be there year-round?
- Is the property graded in a way that allows for a pond or cistern to catch rainwater?

Population Density

During a crisis situation, areas with the highest population densities will experience the most crime, the most social unrest, the highest likelihood for epidemics, and the highest death tolls due to lack of resources and sanitation. When choosing a bug out location, I suggest staying as far away from high-density population areas as possible.

Concealment

You may need to conceal your site during an extreme bug out situation. Having a place that provides adequate resources to conceal your living quarters should be another factor in choosing your location.

- How easy would it be for someone to wander onto your land during a bug out situation?
- Do the natural features of the land help conceal and shelter you or are they an obstacle? This will be a difficult balancing act!
- Can you easily secure and defend the land?

Self-Sufficiency

A location where you can sustain your lifestyle is another important consideration for a bug out property. From having enough sunlight to support a solar system to picking a location that provides a good amount of firewood to heat your home, the ability to sustain your lifestyle needs to be one of the top concerns on your checklist. While these considerations may not be important during short-term evacuation situations, if you're going to spend the money on a secondary shelter, you might as well do it right and prepare for long-term situations as well.

Natural Resources

Consider the area's natural resources when selecting a bug out property:

- How easy is it to grow food on your land?
- Does the area support a population of wild animals for hunting?
- Can you easily raise livestock on the land?

Cost of Living

Unfortunately, most areas of the world are set up in a way that ensures you never really own your property. When considering your location, the cost of living needs to be factored into your plan. Property taxes, cost of local goods, and your ability to keep up with your payments are all things that must be considered.

Zoning Issues

Make sure you thoroughly investigate local zoning ordinances and find out exactly what you can and can't build, what permits are needed, and how much trouble local zoning officials have been to local residents.

BUG OUT BAGS: YOUR LIFELINE DURING AN EVACUATION

Most people who have a basic understanding of survival and preparedness understand the need for a good bug out bag. It's probably one of the most talked-about items on survival websites and is something that has become a bit of an iconic symbol for preppers and survivalists.

If you've never heard the term "bug out bag," it's basically a bag filled with everything you need to survive an extended period away from home. It's something you can grab at a moment's notice should a disaster or emergency situation occur that would require you to immediately evacuate your home. It is an essential part of your evacuation planning.

Evaluating Your Bug Out Bag Needs

As with all types survival gear, there is no one-size-fits-all bug out bag solution. Having a good plan is really the only way to get started. In order to know what items you need to pack, you need to consider the following:

What are the most likely disaster situations you will face? Being prepared for anything means knowing exactly what situations you are preparing for. Before you buy any piece of gear for your bag, figure out what disaster situations you'll most likely face. This will give you a good idea of what you need to pack, how long you need to pack for, and how much gear you will likely need.

What threats will you face during the evacuation? Understanding what threats you'll face along the way is a crucial part of the bug out planning phase. Your threat assessment will help you figure out which items you need to pack, and which items you can do without. I highly advise performing the threat assessment and SWOT analysis, as described in chapter one, before putting anything in your bag.

Who will be traveling with you? Do they have any special needs or medical conditions that need to be addressed? Do they have their own bag filled with gear, and will that gear complement your own? This can help you determine what you need and what you can share with your companions.

Are you actually prepared to bug out? It may sound like a silly question, but I don't think people realize what it's going to take to survive in a real-life bug out situation. It's one thing to talk about bugging out; it's another thing to carry your gear ten to fifteen miles (sixteen to twenty-four kilometers) a day in dangerous and unforgiving conditions. You need to consider your overall physical ability, and if it's a problem, address it now.

Do you need more than one bag? Since you have no way of knowing exactly when and where a disaster will strike, you might want to consider having a bag at home, at your office, and in your vehicle.

ESSENTIAL GEAR FOR BUG OUT BAGS

Water, food, shelter, and protection are the most important things you can focus on when deciding what gear you need to take in a bug out bag. They are the fundamental building blocks to any good bag and should be the foundation that the rest of your gear is built off of.

Water

While some of the items on this list may be considered optional, this is one survival category that's definitely a necessity. Simply put, without it you're dead!

Gallon of water per day. While your exact needs will depend on a number of factors, including your environment, activity level, and overall health, a good rule of thumb is to carry a gallon of water per day, per person.

Water bottles. Having a way to carry and store water is essential to your survival. I recommend carrying an aluminum or steel single-wall canteen for its ability to carry and boil water right in the bottle.

Water filter. In my opinion a good hiking water filter is another important piece of gear. It helps you cut down on your overall water weight and gives you the ability to purify even the most disgusting sources of water.

Food

While food probably won't become a top priority in a short-term emergency situation, it is something that needs to be considered. Survival situations are stressful, and if you end up having to travel on foot, you're going to need the extra energy.

When it comes to choosing the right type of survival foods, keep in mind that you will need far more calories during a bug out situation than on a regular day. Energy bars, trail mix, nuts, and seeds are all things that take up little room in your pack but deliver an enormous amount of calories, protein, essential fats, and energy-producing nutrients.

Just make sure you rotate the food out of your packs every couple of months, especially if you keep a bag in the trunk of your vehicle where extreme temperatures can cause food to spoil much quicker.

Shelter

Hyperthermia (high body temperature) or hypothermia (low body temperature) can set in very fast, so having a way to protect yourself from the elements is a top priority. The type of shelter you choose will depend on your situation, your environment, and your overall ability to improvise shelter from local materials, but in general there are a few things you should consider packing:

Clothing. Although some people might not consider clothing to be shelter, I believe it's one of the most important items in this category. In a survival situation the clothes on your back, combined with what's in your bag, will be your primary source of shelter and protection. Clothing is your first line of defense against the elements and should never be overlooked.

Portable shelters. Some of the most common items include a small tent, a lightweight tarp, sleeping bags, a bivy bag, and even plain old plastic sheeting.

Insulation. In a survival situation, knowing how to properly insulate yourself and your shelter can mean the difference between life and death. Blankets, towels, foam, plastic sheeting, and clothes can all be used in a pinch to add insulation to your clothing or shelter.

Protection

Personal protection is an important but often overlooked bug out category. The great thing about this category is the items serve dual purposes, and in my opinion that's an important factor when choosing any piece of survival gear. From hunting when things go really bad to protecting yourself from wild animals, criminals, and anything that wants to do you harm along the way, a gun is one of the most important things you can carry in your bag.

TRAIN WITH YOUR GEAR

The key to building the perfect bug out bag is continuous testing and improvement. You can have the best gear that money can buy, but if you fail to learn how to use that gear, you might as well fill your bag full of bubble gum because it's going to give you the same benefit during an emergency situation.

If you don't know how to use your gear, don't bother packing a bag. It's really that simple; your life depends on your training, not your gear! The key to survival is knowledge, testing, and training. Take the time and learn how to use your equipment in a real-world setting. Reading about survival is one thing; knowing how to use survival skills and gear in a crisis situation can only be achieved through experience and rigorous training.

BUG OUT BAGS FOR KIDS

While children may not be able to carry a lot of weight, they still need to have their own bug out bags. Individual bug out bags for each family member, no matter how young, are essential. Natural disasters are extremely stressful situations that can severely impact a child's state of mind and mental well-being. It's extremely important for your child to feel as safe and secure as possible during times of crisis. Having his or her own personalized bug out bag, filled with familiar items and comfort foods, can be a lifesaver during a disaster scenario where you may have to leave the comfort of your home.

With children, comfort items are a top priority to ensure their overall mental health during a time of crisis. While I generally don't like to make gear lists, I make an exception when it comes to children.

Basic Survival Items for Kids

While the most important items should always be carried in an adult's bags, I believe involving children in the packing process gives them a sense of power that's important to their mental health. That's why carrying some basic survival items is something that should be included when planning the contents of their bag.

These survival items are appropriate for pretty much all age levels:

- flashlight
- emergency whistle (clipped to the outside of pack so they can easily find it if they become separated from you)
- laminated emergency contact list with name, home address, and telephone numbers
- pre-paid cell phone
- extra socks, pair of gloves, and knit hat or bandana (depending on your climate)
- adhesive bandages and age-appropriate first aid gear
- small bottle of hand sanitizer

Comfort Items

Remember, survival is largely a mental game, and with children this is even more the case. Make sure the comfort items you select are lightweight, age appropriate, and familiar to them:

- stuffed animal
- a few small, lightweight toys
- playing cards or travel-size games
- baseball or a small football
- harmonica or something that makes noise
- MP3 player or small electronic game device
- hard candy
- bubble gum
- sugar packets
- trail mix
- drink mix packets

Remember, a kid's bug out bag is not meant to be an adult's bug out bag. Its sole purpose is to provide comfort to your child during a stressful situation and give him or her a feeling of control. With younger children, comfort items are a top priority and will help to ensure their overall stability throughout the crisis.

Make sure you customize the bag for your child's age, personality, and overall fitness level.

PREPPING YOUR VEHICLE FOR SURVIVAL

During disasters that require you to evacuate, vehicle preparedness becomes even more important as your vehicle will probably be your primary means of getting out of town.

Staying on top of your vehicle's regular preventive maintenance needs including tune-ups, oil changes, battery checks, and tire rotations goes a long way toward preventing problems. But to really be prepared, you need to take vehicle-related safety just as seriously as any other part of your preparedness planning. For example, according to the National Weather Service, 70 percent of all winter storm-related injuries result from vehicle accidents. If that doesn't show you how important vehicle safety issues are, I don't know what will.

Before you hit the roads, there are a number of things you want to do to ensure your safety.

Regular Preventive Maintenance

The first step in being prepared is trying to prevent problems before they start. With vehicle safety, that starts with making sure you stay up-to-date on your vehicle's regular preventive maintenance.

Regular preventive maintenance is probably the single most important thing you can do to ensure your safety while out on the road. While gimmicks used by a lot of unscrupulous mechanics and oil change shops are nothing more than a waste of money, there are some things you need to do to make sure your vehicle is in proper working order.

Do your own inspection. While it's important to routinely have your vehicle checked by a good certified mechanic, you should also have a basic understanding of how your vehicle works and be able to catch anything that looks out of the ordinary. Every couple of weeks, give your vehicle a good once-over, checking fluid levels, tire wear and air pressure, and looking for leaks.

Check your windshield wipers. It may seem relatively unimportant, but having a faulty set of windshield wipers can severely impact your vision during a storm. Your visibility during summer and winter storms relies on having a good working set of windshield wipers and a full reservoir of windshield wiper fluid (during the winter months, switch to a non-freeze wiper fluid formula).

Know when to call a professional. If during your routine inspection you find anything that looks damaged or out of the ordinary, it's a good idea to have your vehicle checked by a certified mechanic. Putting off preventive maintenance or obvious problems like defective tires, leaks, or weird sounds will inevitably lead to problems that could jeopardize the safety of you and your family.

Carry Your Evacuation Plans and Get Home Bags

A backup copy of your evacuation plan, get home plan, and communication plan should be inside your vehicle at all times. When traveling anywhere, you need to be prepared for the possibility of running into danger. Your plans and supplies will do you no good if they aren't with you when you need them.

Invest in a Good Emergency Road Kit

Just like most prepackaged survival kits, most of the commercially available emergency road kits are complete garbage. They are usually filled with cheaply made tools or equipment that does very little to help during an actual emergency.

I suggest taking the time to build your own handpicked emergency road kit and fill it with the items you need to survive roadside emergencies and breakdowns. The kit should take into account where you most often travel and the local weather conditions you'll most likely face. Routinely inspect your kit and rotate items in and out as the seasons change or when you travel to areas with different considerations and threats.

Some items you may want to consider including:

- cell phone charger
- spare fuses
- tire pumps, patches, and a can of Fix-A-Flat
- jack and tire iron or four-way tool to remove tire
- properly inflated spare tire (preferably full size)
- extra oil, antifreeze, and vehicle fluids
- gas can (do not store gasoline inside a vehicle, unless it is strapped down in the bed of a pickup truck or securely attached to the back of a vehicle; storing gasoline inside a vehicle can be deadly)
- jumper cables and/or an emergency car battery jump starter
- spare hoses and fan belts
- a shovel and a piece or carpet or traction material
- fire extinguisher
- flashlight

Vehicle Preparedness Considerations

Never let your gas fall below half a tank. During an emergency situation, you may need to get as far away from the threat as possible. Making a habit of never letting your gas fall below half a tank will help ensure you always have enough fuel to make a quick getaway. It also ensures you never run out of gas.

Don't forget survival supplies. It really doesn't matter how far away from home you're traveling; to be prepared for roadside emergencies and disasters that may hit while away from home, you need to keep some basic survival supplies in your vehicle at all times. This means making sure you have the four key items of survival: water, food, shelter, and protection

Invest in a dedicated cell phone charger. There aren't many roadways in the world where you can't hit some sort of cell tower, but if your cell phone is out of juice, it does you very little good during an emergency. To be able to always call for help, make sure you invest in a good vehicle cell phone charger.

Install a CB radio. Most truckers still rely on these radios while out on the road. This makes having a good CB radio an important part of being prepared for roadway emergencies. Not only can you receive important road-related alerts during a storm, but in an emergency where cell towers are down, you may be able to get in contact with a helpful trucker or a local truck stop that may be monitoring the radio. (In most areas, channel 19 is the most frequently used channel by truckers. In the United States, channel 9 has been designated by the FCC as an emergency contact channel.)

PART TWO:
Surviving Natural Disasters

"I never thought it would happen here." Sadly, these are the most common words spoken after a natural disaster hits. Even sadder are the countless lives lost every year because people failed to take even the most basic of precautions to prepare themselves for these very common threats.

Natural disasters can happen at any time, anywhere in the world. If you live on this planet, you will more than likely have to deal with one of these threats at some point in your life. There's no escaping them, and ignoring the threat will only compound the problem. Once disaster strikes, the time to prepare is over; the only thing you will be left with are the supplies you have on hand and the knowledge you acquired before the disaster.

Part 2 of this book profiles some of the most common natural disasters including severe thunderstorms, tornadoes, flooding, hurricanes, winter storms, earthquakes, and wildfires. The tips provided in the chapters, combined with the preparedness plans recommended in the previous chapters, will help ensure you have what it takes to survive in the face of these very common threats.

Remember, when disaster strikes you're not going to be able to run out to the local grocery store. You need to be prepared for these threats, and the following tips will help you do just that.

Surviving a Severe Thunderstorm and Tornado

6

At any given moment, there are approximately two thousand thunderstorms happening throughout the world. That adds up to a whopping sixteen million storms every year. While I personally love a good thunderstorm, they can be dangerous, and under the right conditions, cause huge amounts of property damage and loss of vital infrastructure. They also have the potential to kill.

HOW DANGEROUS IS THE THREAT?

When compared to something like a hurricane, thunderstorms can seem relatively harmless. Unfortunately, seasonal summer storms can be incredibly dangerous and are responsible for taking numerous lives and causing billions of dollars in property damage every year.

Thunderstorms can produce a wide array of dangerous weather, including flash floods, tornadoes, damaging winds, hail, and dangerous lighting strikes. Lightning can be particularly dangerous and is responsible for a large number of power outages, wildfires, injuries, and deaths every year.

Lightning
- can occur during all types of summer storms
- is responsible for killing an estimated 24,000 people throughout the world each year, and injuring around 240,000 people
- strikes the Earth an average of one hundred times per second
- No outdoor location is safe during a thunderstorm. If a storm is within 10 miles (16 km) of your location, you are at risk of being struck by lightning.

Tornadoes

- can generate winds that exceed 300 miles (483 km) per hour
- can last over an hour
- can leave a path of destruction over a mile (1.6 km) wide and 50 miles (80 km) long

Flooding

- is the number one cause of summer storm-related deaths
- can happen quickly and can easily sweep a person off his or her feet in even a few inches of fast-moving water
- causes more than $5 billion in damage every year

Hail

- is responsible for an estimated one billion dollars in crop and property damages every year
- can be larger than 6 inches (15 cm) in diameter
- can weigh as much as 2¼ pounds (1 kg) and fall at speeds of up to 110 miles (177 km) per hour

ATTRIBUTES OF A THUNDERSTORM

Thunderstorms are most likely to occur during the spring and summer months, with a majority of the storms happening in the afternoon and evening hours. This is because thunderstorms thrive under moist and warm conditions, which are the two most important ingredients in the formation of the unstable air that causes these storms.

- Thunderstorms can occur one at a time, in clusters, or in lines. Just because a storm seems to have passed doesn't necessarily mean you're out of the danger zone.
- Thunderstorms average from 5 to 25 miles (8 to 40 km) in diameter and typically last an average of 20 to 30 minutes.
- The most dangerous thunderstorms are single storms that stay over one location for an extended period of time.

Some signs of an impending storm include

1. **Bizarre animal behavior.** Animals have a sixth sense when it comes to approaching natural disasters and storms; they often become nervous and jittery, and can be excellent predictors of foul weather.
2. **Pops and static on AM radio bands.** If you hear an increase in noise on these bands, it's a pretty good indicator that thunderstorms are near.
3. **A sudden increase in wind**, a strong blast that seemingly comes out of nowhere, or a sudden change in wind direction are all signs of an approaching storm.
4. **Your nose can smell it coming.** Believe it or not, some people are very good at noticing small changes in the air and can even sense moisture or the smell of rain before it arrives.
5. **Watch for red skies and/or dark and billowing clouds.** In general, low-hanging, dark clouds usually indicate storms are on the way.

Summer storms have the potential to be very dangerous, so it's important to take all alerts seriously—especially severe thunderstorm warnings.

UNDERSTAND OFFICIAL WEATHER WARNINGS

Severe Thunderstorm Watch. A watch means the potential for a storm exists, and you need to be on the lookout for bad weather. In general, you can still go about your regular activities, but keep a watchful eye on the sky, and listen for local weather updates.

Severe Thunderstorm Warning. A warning is issued when a thunderstorm is either occurring in the area or the conditions for one have been spotted on radar and weather officials believe a storm is imminent.

Tornado Watch. A watch is issued when there are storms in the area capable of producing a tornado. If a watch is issued, be ready to take action at a moment's notice.

Tornado Warning. A warning is issued when tornadoes have been spotted in the area or conditions for one have been seen on radar and weather officials believe a tornado is imminent. If a warning is issued, take cover immediately.

Every year countless numbers of people are killed or severely injured because they ignored the warnings. When a severe storm or tornado warning is issued, take shelter and listen for local weather updates.

PREPARATIONS TO MAKE BEFORE THE STORM HITS

When it comes to summer storms, recognizing the danger is probably the most important thing you can do to protect yourself and your family. Unfortunately, a countless number of people are killed or injured every year because they underestimated the power of these powerful seasonal storms.

To prepare for a thunderstorm

- Make sure you have a fully stocked emergency kit filled with everything you need to survive an extended power outage. Food, water, first aid kits, flashlights, and extra batteries need to be on hand.
- Designate an area in your home where you and your family will gather during a storm. If at all possible, having a safe room built into your home can provide an extra layer of protection, not only from seasonal thunderstorms but a wide range of threats. If you don't have a safe room, designate an area on the lowest floor of your home away from windows, glass doors and anything that can be broken by strong winds and hail.
- Make sure you invest in a good battery-operated NOAA Weather Radio. These radios can help you stay informed on what's going on and can warn you before a dangerous storm catches you off guard.
- Do a visual inspection of the area around your home. Look for anything that can blow away or cause damage once the wind starts picking up.
- Remove dead trees and damaged branches that could fall and cause injury during a severe storm.
- Install surge protectors inside your home and think about unplugging your valuable electronics ahead of any severe storm.

PROTECTING YOURSELF DURING THE STORM

When the storm is in your area, there are some things you can do to stay safe:

- Avoid touching any electrical appliances that are not attached to surge protectors. Even then you still need to be cautious.
- If driving, look for the safest place to pull off the road. Park and turn on your vehicle's emergency lights. Stay in your vehicle, unless you can safely make your way into a sturdy building.
- Listen to your NOAA Weather Radio or local news for storm-related updates.
- If you can hear thunder, you are technically in the danger zone. When lightning is in the area, there really is no safe place outdoors. As soon as you hear the rumble of thunder, it's time to take shelter and head indoors.
- If you're outside and cannot make it to a safe shelter, take cover in a low-lying area and minimize contact with the ground. Avoid hilltops, open fields, water, high ground, and tall, isolated trees.
- Avoid contact with metal objects such as fences, bleachers, golf clubs, fishing poles, or anything that can attract lightning.

PROTECTING YOURSELF IN THE STORM'S AFTERMATH

As with all natural disasters, after the storm passes you still need to be on alert. There may be other storms in the area, and there are dangers that can be present in the immediate aftermath of the storm.

- Avoid flooded roadways and stay away from storm-damaged areas.
- Continue to listen to local news updates for storm-related information and instructions.
- Be on the lookout for downed power lines. If you see one, immediately report it to the power company, police, or fire department.
- If you lose power, heat-related illness can become a real threat during hot summer months. Stay hydrated, work during cooler hours of the day, and watch for signs of heat illness in yourself and others.

TORNADOES—THE ULTIMATE SUMMER STORM THREAT

Tornadoes are one of the most violent and devastating storms you can face. Their destructive speed and power is unmatched by any other weather phenomenon. Tornado winds have been clocked in excess of 300 miles (483 km) per hour and can leave a path of destruction over 50 miles (80 km) long. They can last from several seconds to over an hour, with the average tornado lasting around five minutes.

How Real Is the Threat?

The level of threat tornadoes pose depends on where you live. Although they are often associated with areas in the central United States, tornadoes can occur in many other parts of the world as well, including Africa, Asia, Australia, Europe, and South America.

Tornadoes most often occur during the spring and summer in the late afternoon or early evening hours during certain types of atmospheric conditions. One of the biggest tornado-related concerns is the speed with which they can develop—sometimes forming without warning. Although tornados can seem to come out of nowhere, forecasters are getting better at predicting when they might occur so you need to take weather-related warnings seriously.

How Dangerous Is the Threat?

In the United States alone, more than one thousand tornadoes are reported every year. The path of destruction can be up to a mile (1.6 km) wide, and in some cases more than 50 miles (80 km) long.

- The strong winds generated by tornadoes can send cars airborne, flattening homes and entire towns, and damaging vital infrastructure.
- Flying debris presents one of the biggest threats during a tornado, which can turn broken glass and debris into lethal projectiles that can easily penetrate a person.
- They can strike quickly, and sometimes without warning.
- They are most often associated with severe thunderstorms but can also accompany tropical storms and hurricanes.

Attributes of a Tornado

The best way to limit your risk is to pay attention to local weather reports. When a tornado watch or warning is issued, you need to take it seriously. Unfortunately, a lot of people tend to ignore these warnings since approximately 70 percent of the ones issued in the United States each year are false alarms. Although the science behind predicting them is far from perfect, when they do hit, these alerts can give you a ten-minute head start and can help you take the proper precautions.

Paying attention to local weather reports can help, but knowing what to watch for can save your life. Here's what you need to watch out for:

- **Dead calm.** it may seem weird, but many times an approaching tornado can cause an intense storm to suddenly seem like it's stopped.
- **Sounds similar to a freight train.** If you hear a continuous low rumbling noise or something that sounds like thunder that doesn't stop, there's a good chance the sound is being caused by an approaching tornado.
- **Rotation in the clouds.** Rotation in the cloud base or whirling debris are often the first signs of a tornado. A cloud of debris can be a sign of trouble, even if a funnel cloud is not visible.
- **Wall clouds.** A wall cloud is often a very telling sign—one that signals trouble is near. Watch for any clouds that appear to extend out below the main cloud line, especially ones that have a blimp-like structure.

What to Do During a Tornado

Take shelter. After a tornado warning has been issued, make your way to a basement or underground shelter. If you don't have access to a basement, head toward an interior room at the lowest level of your home.

Stay away from doors and windows. Closets and hallways are going to be far safer than a room with windows or doors to the outside.

If you're outside

- Immediately make your way to the closest sturdy shelter.
- If you can't make it to a shelter, look for the lowest level in the area and

immediately move toward it. Something like a culvert or roadway ditch is going to be a much better option than an open field.

- Do not get under a highway overpass or bridge. Despite what the movies may show, these areas are extremely dangerous during a tornado and can create a deadly wind tunnel. You are far safer in a low, flat location.
- Cover your head with a coat, blanket or any other cushioning you can find.

Preparing a Tornado Safe Room

If you live in a high-risk tornado area, seriously consider building a safe room where your family can seek refuge during a storm. The best place to build your shelter is underground. If you don't have the ability to build an underground shelter, other areas you may want to consider include:

- your basement; shelters built below ground level will offer the highest level of protection
- under a concrete slab or garage floor
- an interior room or closet on the ground floor of your home

Your shelter should be built to withstand high winds, and should be filled with emergency supplies and a way to communicate with the outside world. Other considerations include:

- Anchor the shelter to resist lifting or overturning.
- Use high-strength building materials that will stand up against falling and flying debris.
- Making sure the shelter is properly ventilated and cannot be obstructed by debris.

(7) Surviving a Flood

Floods are among the most common and destructive natural disasters we face. Flash floods can easily inundate an area after only a few minutes or hours of intense rainfall. Floods have the potential to cause untold amounts of damage.

HOW REAL IS THE THREAT?

While the topography of some areas makes them more prone to flooding, keep in mind that any location that receives rainfall has the potential to flood. Although a majority of these floods are storm related, there is a growing concern among intelligence officials that terrorists could target dams and levee systems in order to cause devastating floods. If you live or work near a dam or levee system, you need to be especially prepared for the possibility of an unexpected flooding.

HOW DANGEROUS IS THE THREAT?

Worldwide, flash floods and flooding are the number one thunderstorm-related cause of death. Most of the danger lies in the speed and force at which the floodwater moves. Most people simply don't realize how dangerous it actually is.

- As little as 6 inches (15 cm) of floodwater is enough to knock down a full-grown adult.
- 18 inches (46 cm) of floodwater can create enough force to wash away a car.

In the United States, floods cause more damage than any other type of severe-weather-related event, costing an average of $5 billion each year.

HOW TO MINIMIZE THE THREAT

Surviving a flood requires preparation. That means knowing what the threats are and finding out whether or not your home is in a known flood zone.

Unfortunately, because of an increased threat of terrorism, many governments have moved to restrict maps from showing areas that could be inundated by floodwaters. This makes it hard for average citizens to fully understand the dangers they may face.

Although many of these flood zone maps are now hard to come by, contacting your state's dam safety agency or your local emergency management officials can help you understand the potential dangers in your neighborhood. Many times these local agencies can provide a wealth of knowledge, and they're more likely to share their information with the public.

Another important part of preparing for floods is having a way to find out when they're coming. I recommend buying a good NOAA Weather Radio. In North America, NOAA Weather Radios receive alerts from a nationwide network of radio stations that broadcast emergency alerts from the National Weather Service. These alerts are broadcast 24/7, and they are one of the best ways to receive warnings and stay on top of potential storm-related threats.

HOW CAN YOU PREPARE FOR THE THREAT?

We've already discussed how deadly even 6 inches (15 cm) of floodwater can be. If a flood is on its way or already forming, you need to be prepared to evacuate immediately.

- **Bug out bags.** Since flash floods can quickly overtake an area, it's important to have a bug out bag filled with emergency supplies that you can grab at a moment's notice.
- **Plan and practice.** Make sure everyone in your family is on board with your emergency plan including evacuation routes, communication plans, and emergency meet-up points (all discussed in chapter two.)
- **Find high ground.** In the case of immediate flooding, where you may become unable to evacuate, it's important to know exactly where the highest areas are in your neighborhood.

PREPARING YOUR HOME

- **Have sandbags ready to go.** If you live in a flood zone, sandbags and shovels should be part of your preparedness stockpile. Check with your local city or state government, as most municipalities will have sand piles available to the public.
- **Elevate important items and appliances.** If you live in a high-risk area, you need to elevate anything that's important to you. You also need to raise electrical panels, water heaters, and your furnace to protect them from floodwater.
- **Install check valves.** Installing check valves can prevent floodwater and sewage from backing up into your home.
- **Know how to turn off your utilities.** If floodwater is approaching your home, you may need to cut off your utilities at the source. If you don't know how, consult with your local utility company to learn how to disconnect all incoming services during an emergency.

HOW CAN YOU SURVIVE THE AFTERMATH?
Don't Let Your Guard Down

Even in areas where floodwater has receded, there still may be a cause for concern. Roads can become weakened by floodwater and can easily collapse under the weight of a car.

- Watch for downed power lines.
- Pay attention to flooded roadways after the water recedes.
- Stay away from areas that are prone to mudslides.

Avoid Floodwater

After a flood, you need to stay away from any standing water. There's a pretty good chance most of the floodwater will be contaminated by oil, gasoline, chemicals, bacteria, and even raw sewage.

- Avoid walking, touching, or swimming in floodwater.
- Stay away from all moving water. Remember, six inches of water is all it takes to knock over a full-grown man.

- Don't drive through areas that are flooded. It doesn't take much to sweep a car off the road, and it's difficult to gauge the depth of the water on the roadway. Even if you don't get swept away, you may seriously damage your car by filling it with floodwater. If in doubt, turn around or find an alternate route.

Check Your Home Before Reentering

After the floodwaters recede, you still need to stay on guard even when reentering your home.

- Make a visual inspection of your home before reentering the structure.
- Look for signs of structural damage such as cracks, or if the house seems like it's sitting lower than usual.
- Check for loose or downed power lines. Electric currents can still run through downed lines, sending electricity through any standing water.
- Smell the air around you. If you notice the smell of gas, there is a good chance the gas lines have been compromised. Immediately call your local gas utility, and have them send someone to inspect the area.

Water and electricity don't mix. If there is standing water inside your home, you increase your risk of electrocution. If possible, before entering your home shut off all power at your home's breaker panel. If your breaker box is inside your home, or surrounded by water, *do not attempt to turn off your power.* Call your electric utility to shut off power at the meter, then you can safely turn off the power at your breaker box.

Surviving a Hurricane

Hurricanes are one of the most destructive and potentially deadly natural disasters you can face. From powerful winds that can wreak havoc on your property to torrential rains and damaging storm surges that can devastate entire coastal communities, hurricanes can unleash a wide array of dangerous hazards.

During a hurricane, buildings, roadways, vital infrastructure, and other structures can be severely damaged or destroyed. If you live near a coastline or in an area that can be affected by hurricanes, you need to take the threat seriously.

ATTRIBUTES OF A HURRICANE

Throughout the world, hurricanes are known by a number of names:

- **Hurricanes.** North Atlantic (including Caribbean and Gulf of Mexico), Eastern and Central North Pacific, and Western South Pacific
- **Typhoons.** Western Northern Pacific and the China Sea
- **Tropical Cyclones.** Arabian Sea/Northern Indian Ocean, the South Indian Ocean, and the Coral Sea/South Pacific
- **Tropical Cyclones/Willy-Willy.** Australia

The strength of the storm is classified by something known as the Saffir–Simpson hurricane wind scale, which is split into five categories distinguished by the strengths of sustained winds.

- Category 1: 74-95 mph (119-153 km/h)
- Category 2: 96-110 mph (154-177 km/h)
- Category 3: 111-129 mph (178-208 km/h)
- Category 4: 130-156 mph (209-251 km/h)
- Category 5: over 157 mph (252 km/h)

HOW REAL IS THE THREAT?

Hurricanes are relatively common. On average, the world sees somewhere around 70 to 110 every year.

Hurricanes are the single most powerful atmospheric phenomenon we face. The storms can produce torrential rains, spawn tornadoes, cause major flooding, and can even whip up winds that exceed 155 miles (249 km) per hour.

Hurricanes are not something that should be taken lightly. Even a small tropical storm can produce heavy rain and winds that can devastate a community. From downed power lines and flash floods to storm surges that can be as high as 20 feet (6 m) and 100 miles (161 km) wide, a hurricane can create a path of destruction that can cause billions of dollars in damage and kill numerous people.

Man-Made Threats in Response to Hurricanes

Weather isn't the only factor wreaking havoc during a hurricane. The general public's response to the storm will also pose potential threats and difficulties.

Stores will run out of supplies almost immediately. As soon as a hurricane warning is issued, people are going to be frantically rushing to buy supplies. Because most people are completely unprepared to face even a small-scale disaster, the grocery stores will be stripped bare in a matter of hours.

Electronic payments will go down. Our reliance on modern technology, especially electronic payments, has left us extremely vulnerable to natural disasters. During most hurricanes, the affected areas often lose power for days, sometimes even weeks. That means you need to be prepared to pay for things without using your debit and credit cards.

Criminals will prey on the weak. Criminals love to exploit natural disasters. While you're paying attention to the chaos the storm is causing, they're plotting how they can use it to their advantage. You need to be prepared to defend yourself from looters and other criminals who may be looking to do more than just steal your property.

Watch out for the government. It's sad, but as we've seen during previous hurricanes, you may have to watch out for your own government. During Hurricane

Katrina, New Orleans residents had their homes raided and their legal firearms confiscated in the name of "protecting" the public.

WHAT CAN YOU DO TO MINIMIZE THE THREAT?

- Before hurricane seasons starts, purchase marine-grade plywood at least ⅝-inch (2 cm) thick and cut coverings for all your windows. Paint the location of the window (e.g., left living room) on each covering so you can quickly put the coverings on before a storm.
- Prior to landfall, secure everything that's outside your home that could turn into a dangerous projectile during the storm. Strap down or bring in any anything that you don't want to fly away.
- If you expect major flooding it might be a good idea to temporarily turn off your utilities at the main switches or valves. Also consider placing sandbags around your home before the storm makes landfall.

If you decide to stay in your home during a hurricane, you need to be able to survive for at least fourteen days without food, water, or power. The government often recommends that you need at least seventy-two hours' worth of supplies, but based on past hurricanes and natural disasters, expecting to be back up and running within seventy-two hours is completely unrealistic.

Don't wait until a hurricane is on the way to stock up on supplies you will need. Panic buying will ensure you won't be able to get everything you need. Stock up on these supplies now, so you are ready well ahead of the storm.

- Think about what things you would take on a camping trip, one where you had no access to power or water. These are the type of things you'll want to stock up on, because you'll probably be camping out in your home for at least a couple of days following the storm.
- Lighting is a top concern. Candles, lanterns and flashlights are all essential during a hurricane. Make sure you have multiple methods of lighting your home, and don't forget to stock up on extra batteries.
- A generator makes things easier and provides an extra layer of safety during a power outage. Remember to keep it away from your home and windows so the exhaust fumes don't blow back into your home.

- Having canned food that can be eaten right out of the can is always a good idea. Not only can it be eaten without cooking, but it can make life easier and give you less to worry about after the storm. Just make sure to have a couple non-electric can openers on hand, or buy the cans with easy-open pop tops.

STAYING SAFE DURING A HURRICANE

Unlike tornadoes or flash floods, hurricanes will give more notice before blowing through your area. Pay attention to weather reports and warnings so you can act as quickly as possible.

Evacuate

The best way to stay safe during a hurricane is to evacuate the storm-threatened area. In my opinion, staying to "protect your stuff" is not worth losing your life. In the case of a major hurricane, it's often best to heed evacuation warnings—especially if you live in an area that's prone to flooding.

- **Bug out bags.** Keep these packed and ready to go so you can grab them and go at a moment's notice.
- **Plan and practice.** Make sure everyone in your family is on board with your emergency plan including evacuation routes, communication plans, and emergency meet-up points (all discussed in chapter two.)
- **Don't wait until the last-minute.** You could end up stuck in traffic on the highway when the storm hits.

Sheltering in During the Storm

If you decide not to evacuate, take shelter in small interior rooms, closets, or areas without windows that are preferably on the lower levels of your home. If you live in a high-rise building, you need to find somewhere else to go. The higher off the ground you are during the storm, the worse the winds will become.

If you don't have a large amount of water on hand, fill up as many containers as you can before the storm hits. Tap water usually becomes unsafe after a hurricane and you'll want to have as much water on hand as you can store. Pots, pans, and even your bathtub can be a great way to store extra water.

Beware of the calm in the middle of the storm. A lot of people get into trouble because they drop their guard when it seems like things have calmed down. Remember, when the eye of the storm is overhead it can look like the storm has passed. In reality, there's more to come and what's coming can often be worse than what's already passed.

HOW TO SURVIVE THE AFTERMATH

Unfortunately, once the winds subside, you're still not out of danger. In fact, the aftermath may be the most dangerous part of the storm you will face. From bacteria-laden floodwater to looters looking to take advantage of an already bad situation, you need to keep your guard up until things return to normal. After the storm

- **Avoid floodwater.** Floodwater often contains things that are hazardous to your health. From raw sewage, oil and gasoline, to other potential dangers like downed power lines, the last thing you want to do is go wading through floodwater.

- **Monitor your weather radio.** Make sure you monitor the situation so you know if things are getting better or worse. Knowledge is power, so make sure you know what's going on around you.

- **Be aware of looters.** Unfortunately there are some people in this world who thrive off of chaos. In the immediate aftermath of any significant disaster, especially one that causes large areas to lose power, you may have to deal with looters.

(9) Surviving a Winter Storm

Winter storms can be extremely powerful. Heavy snowfall, ice accumulation, and extreme cold can cripple entire regions. They have the potential to cause large amounts of property damage, disrupt essential services and utilities, and can be deadly for those who aren't prepared.

HOW REAL IS THE THREAT?

The level of the threat depends on where you live, but at some point, regardless of where you live, you will probably be affected by winter weather. Even in the Southwestern deserts of the United States, where most people wouldn't expect to be affected, freak winter storms can cause a wide range of problems, specifically because they are so uncommon and so many people will be unprepared.

Winter storms can cause a number of problems, including

- **Icy roads.** Icy roads and blinding blizzard conditions can make our roadways extremely dangerous. One of the greatest hazards during winter storms comes from people driving during dangerous conditions Over 70 percent of winter-storm-related deaths occur in automobiles.
- **Power outages.** Ice, wind, and falling trees can take down power lines. During freezing cold temperatures this can be extremely dangerous and puts people at the risk of hypothermia due to prolonged exposure to cold temperatures. It also exposes you to the risk of freezing and bursting pipes in your home.
- **Hypothermia and frostbite.** During extreme winter weather, hypothermia and frostbite can set in very quickly. Exposure to the cold can be extremely dangerous and needs to be taken seriously.

PROTECTING YOUR PIPES

Winter weather can wreak havoc on your pipes. Extreme cold can cause water to quickly freeze and expand inside unprotected pipes. If the frozen water expands enough, pipes can easily burst, causing serious problems.

- Vulnerable pipes should be wrapped with insulation or pipe sleeves. During extreme cold you can also use blankets or towels to wrap exposed pipes.
- Cracks or holes in exterior walls, especially those near pipes, should be filled with caulking.
- Keep garage doors closed if water supply lines are located inside the garage.
- Leaving cabinet doors open can help circulate warm air around the pipes.
- Leaving your faucets on so they slowly drip can help relieve pressure and prevent pipes from bursting during extreme cold weather.
- If you suspect a frozen pipe; open the faucet and slowly apply warm air with a household hair dryer. Never use an open flame to thaw a frozen pipe.

WHAT CAN YOU DO TO PREPARE FOR THE THREAT?

Keep in mind that a winter storm can be just as dangerous and deadly as any other type of weather phenomenon. It can also knock out power or cause you to become stuck in your home for days, maybe even weeks.

Having a good supply of food, water, and emergency supplies is an essential part of being prepared for winter storms. You may be unable to leave your house for an extended period of time.

Stock up well ahead of time to avoid the problems of panic buying that precedes any storm:

- Stock up on extra bottled water.
- Make sure you have ready-to-eat foods that can be eaten without having to cook them.
- Make sure you have an ample supply of any medications you are taking.

Heavy snow and ice frequently damage power lines, so you need to be prepared for the possibility of power outages:

- Stock up on candles, flashlights, oil-burning lamps, and extra batteries.
- Consider buying an emergency generator. It can be a lifesaver during the cold winter months.
- Stock up on cat litter, road salt, or bags of sand to add traction on sidewalks and driveways.

To keep yourself safe and warm, consider stocking up on

- extra blankets and quilts, sleeping bags, winter clothing, hats, and winter coats
- space blankets and chemical hand/body warmers
- extra firewood for your fireplace
- portable space heaters, propane heaters, or kerosene heaters
- carbon monoxide detector (This is extremely important and should not be overlooked; if used improperly some of these heating methods can cause a buildup of deadly carbon monoxide.)

STAYING SAFE DURING A WINTER STORM

Stay Home

Battling icy snowy roads is not fun; in fact, it can be downright dangerous. If you don't need to go out, play it safe and stay home. If a storm is on its way, don't wait for the weather to start before you start for home. Stay home prior to storm fall or leave early so you don't get stranded.

Watch for Signs of Hypothermia

Hypothermia occurs when the body's core temperature drops to a point where normal functions are impaired. During the winter this can happen fairly quickly, so it's important to watch for things like uncontrollable shivering, mental changes and confusion, memory loss, slurred speech, labored breathing, drowsiness, and muscle impairment. If you or someone around you starts to experience any of these symptoms, it's extremely important to remove any wet clothing, warm the center of the body, and begin to drink warm, non-alcoholic beverages.

Stock Your Vehicle

If you're heading out during a winter storm, don't overlook the importance of bringing along some basic emergency supplies. Most of the items you would pack in a winter bug out bag should be carried inside your vehicle during hazardous winter excursions.

- **Check your vehicle's fluid levels.** Antifreeze, oil, and transmission fluids should all be checked and topped off before you leave. Also, make sure you have enough windshield washer fluid in the reservoir and make sure it's rated for freezing temperatures.
- **Check your battery.** If your battery is over three years old, it's probably a good idea to have it checked before heading out on a long road trip. Most auto parts stores offer free battery checks, and they only take a couple of minutes of your time.
- **Check your air pressure.** Underinflation is the leading cause of tire failure; in the winter this can be a huge problem. When the temperatures start to dip, cold weather can cause your tires to become dangerously underinflated. For every ten-degree drop in temperature, your tires can lose as much as 1 pound per square inch (PSI) of pressure.
- **Give your vehicle a final road inspection before leaving.** Before leaving, give your vehicle a final once-over. Check for leaks, worn-out hoses, cracks in the belts, and make sure to inspect your tire tread. If anything looks out of whack, now is the time to take care of it.

DRIVING IN SLICK CONDITIONS

The best way to stay safe during severe weather that has turned the roadways into a slippery driving nightmare is to stay home. If you are forced to drive under these conditions, there are a few things you need to do to increase your safety:

- **Be prepared.** Have your tires, brakes, and wipers checked before the storm.

HOW TO STOP A VEHICLE WHEN THE BRAKES FAIL

Having your brakes go out while driving can be downright terrifying. While it's rare, it does happen, so knowing how to respond during that situation can mean the difference between life and death.

If you find yourself unable to stop while driving, the following steps should help:

1. Immediately downshift to a lower gear. Downshifting into a lower gear allows your engine to slow down your vehicle and could give you enough time to find a safe place to pull over. Slowly make your way through the lower gears one at a time, allowing the engine to slow the vehicle. (In vehicles with an automatic transmission, look for the highest gear on your automatic gear shift and then work your way down to 1.)

2. Check for obstructions. This may sound stupid, but something as simple as a cell phone that fell off the dash could be causing your problems. Use your foot to make sure nothing is wedged behind your brake pedal. If you feel anything, kick it out of the way and slowly apply the break pedal.

3. Pump the brakes. If you have regular brakes, quickly pumping the brakes can sometimes build up brake fluid pressure giving you enough brake to come to a stop. If you have anti-lock brakes, your vehicle does the pumping for you so just firmly press down on the brake.

- **Eliminate all driving distractions.** Stay off the cell phone, put down the munchies, and keep your radio turned down or off.
- **Slow down.** During slick driving conditions, your vehicle needs three times the normal distance to stop.
- **Accelerate, turn, and brake slowly.** During slick driving conditions, everything needs to be done slower. Applying the gas slowly to acceler- ate is the best method for regaining traction and avoiding skids. Don't

4. Slowly engage your emergency brake. If pumping the brakes didn't work, slowly engage your vehicle's parking/emergency brake and be prepared for the vehicle to skid.

5. Grab the attention of anyone in your path. If nothing is working, you need to clear the path. Honk, flash your headlights, and turn on your hazard lights so everyone can get out of your way.

6. Look for something soft or something that can slow you down. If all else fails you may be forced to find something that can slow you down. On steep mountainous roads, look for an emergency runaway truck ramp, which will be filled with sand and gravel and is meant to slow down vehicles that have lost the ability to brake. Walls, guardrails, and brush can all be used to gently scrape the side of your vehicle, using the friction to slow the car down enough until you roll to a complete stop.

If a collision becomes unavoidable, stay calm and try to find something that will give. A fence or a bunch of bushes is going to be a much better option than a solid wall or a large, solid tree. Stay with the car and try to keep as much control over what's going on as possible. Taking your hands off the wheel and giving up is going to make the situation much worse.

try to get moving in a hurry. And take time to slow down for a stoplight. Remember: It takes longer to slow down on icy roads.

- **Know when to call it quits.** If driving becomes too risky, you need to know when to call it quits and find a safe place to pull off the road. If conditions are bad, be prepared to stop and wait the storm out at a hotel or a truck stop until the roads are in safe traveling condition.

DRIVING OUT OF A SKID

Knowing how to get out of a skid is essential when driving under slick conditions. If you feel your vehicle losing control,

1. **Take your feet off the pedals.** Most people immediately go for the brake pedal when they start to slide out; this is a huge mistake. Hitting the gas or the brake pedal is only going to make things worse.

2. **Steer where you want to go.** One of the biggest mistakes people make is trying to overcompensate by jerking the wheel into the direction they are skidding. The second your vehicle starts sliding, look toward the direction you want to go and steer your vehicle directly where you want to go. It's important to put your eyes on where you want to go because your hands follow your eyes automatically.

3. **Gently apply the brakes or the gas.** Depending on the direction of your skid, after you regain some control you may need to gently apply the brakes or the accelerator. If your front wheels are sliding, gently apply the brake. If your rear wheels are sliding, gently apply the gas.

FREEING A STUCK VEHICLE

Getting stuck in the snow, mud, or in off-road gravel can be a real problem, especially if you're stuck miles from help or during a storm where rescue could take some time. But if you're prepared, getting your vehicle out is often only a matter of being able to get enough traction.

If you find yourself in a position where your vehicle is stuck, here are some things you can do to free your vehicle. Keep in mind many of these things require a bit of preplanning, so make sure your vehicle is stocked with what you need.

Supplies That Can Help

- **Carry some extra weight.** While it may not be super fuel-efficient, if you're traveling in off-road areas, or during stormy or icy conditions, packing a couple of sandbags can help give you some added traction when you're stuck.

- **Carry a shovel and traction pad.** Add a shovel and a piece of carpet or traction pad to your supplies and you should have everything you need to free yourself from most situations. The shovel can help you create an easy path out, and the carpet can help give you enough traction so your wheels don't spin and dig you in deeper.

- **Carry a board and a heavy-duty tire jack.** If your vehicle is really stuck, you may have to jack it up before placing your traction pad under the tires. Make sure the ground is firm. If it's not, place your jack on a board to add stability before you jack it up.

Techniques to Keep In Mind

- **Slow and steady.** Hitting the gas will likely make the situation worse. The moment you get stuck, you need to stop, remain calm, and slowly give the vehicle some gas. Give your vehicle a little gas and then let off. Keep repeating, as the rocking motion will help free the vehicle. If you feel the vehicle becoming more stuck, stop and think about adding traction.

- **It's all about adding traction.** If you're stuck without a traction mat, look for anything that can help you add traction under the tires. Large branches, rocks, and anything that can add traction should be placed in front of your drive wheels. Just make sure you shovel a path before placing your traction materials down.

- **Rock the vehicle.** Once you have created a clear path, added traction to the ground, and are ready to attempt to free the vehicle, resist the urge to floor it. Instead, use your vehicle's gears to help slowly rock the vehicle back and forth. Shifting between drive and reverse can help free most stuck vehicles; just make sure you shift directions when the wheels start to spin. Also, don't go crazy; the last thing you want is to fry your vehicle's transmission.

- **Let a little air out of the tires.** As a last resort, letting a little bit of air out of your tires will give them a wider footprint, creating less resistance and giving you a better chance of freeing your stuck vehicle. Just keep an eye on how much air you're letting out, because freeing your vehicle isn't going to help if you have flat tires.

Surviving an Earthquake

Earthquakes can strike at any time, almost anywhere in the world. They are probably one of the most feared natural disasters, and their unpredictable nature makes them one of the hardest to prepare for.

HOW REAL IS THE THREAT?

The extent of the threat depends on a number of factors, but the two key factors that usually determine how big the quake can be are your geographical location and the geographical makeup of the ground in your area.

If you live in a known earthquake zone, or in an area where the ground increases the destructive power of an earthquake, you need to take the threat seriously. Exactly when the Big One will hit can't be predicted, but you can be sure that at some point it will happen, so you need to take precautions.

HOW ARE EARTHQUAKE MAGNITUDES MEASURED?

While there are a number of different methods for calculating the size of an earthquake, one of the most common methods cited is usually the Richter magnitude scale. Developed in 1935 by Charles Richter, the Richter scale is used to measure the magnitude of most earthquakes, and gives scientists the ability to track and compare the strength of earthquakes at different times and locations.

The Richter scale is based on a base-10 logarithmic scale, meaning for every whole number jump in magnitude the amplitude of the ground motion goes up ten times. So a magnitude 5 quake on the Richter scale would result in ten times the level of ground shaking as a magnitude 4 earthquake (and 31.7 times as much energy would be released). Quakes below 4.9 are considered fairly minor and cause a minimum amount of damage. Quakes that are 5.0 to 5.9 are considered moderate and can cause damage, particularly to poorly constructed structures, but few deaths. Quakes over 6.0 will cause significant damage to even well-constructed buildings, which greatly increases the risk of death and injury.

EARTHQUAKE-RELATED DANGERS

The dangers associated with an earthquake really depend on the size, location, and how long the quake lasts. While earthquakes pose little direct danger to a person, the resulting damage to buildings, vital infrastructure, and roads can make them extremely dangerous. Some earthquake side effects that can be dangerous to people include:

Falling Debris

One of the most immediate dangers from an earthquake comes from falling debris. The shaking from a quake can cause almost anything in your home to fall over, and can even cause glass windows to shatter and ceilings to crumble. Heavy items like large appliances and bookshelves or hutches also present a significant risk to anyone who's near them during the quake.

Damage to Vital Infrastructure

Falling electrical lines, ruptured gas and water lines, and badly damaged road-ways are all common occurrences after a large quake. After an earthquake, stay alert to these hazards, be on the lookout for aftershocks, and stay away from damaged areas.

Collapsing Buildings and Structures

Buildings can be damaged by the shaking itself or by ground displacement that can literally rip a building right in half. Aftershocks can continue to cause struc-tural damage for days, weeks, and even months after the initial quake, adding to a building's instability.

Flooding and Tsunamis

Those who live in low-lying coastal areas need to be aware of tsunamis, which can be triggered by the seismic energy of an earthquake. This was the case after the 2011 Tōhoku Japan earthquake, which generated waves over 100 feet (30 m) high, killing thousands and destroying entire coastal communities.

Not all earthquakes cause tsunamis, but it is a possibility if the quake strikes anywhere near an ocean. If you live in a known tsunami zone, the best thing you can do is evacuate following any sizable earthquake.

Man-made Threats That Follow Earthquakes

While it's impossible to predict an earthquake, there are some things that you can be pretty sure will happen following a large quake:

- **Stores will run out of supplies within hours of the event.** You need to have enough supplies on hand to make it through an extended period of time while stores will be closed, utilities will be down, and supply chains will be interrupted.
- **Your credit and debit cards will be worthless.** Damage to infrastructure and local power grids could make electronic payments difficult. You'll need to have cash on hand to pay for everything.
- **Be on the lookout for looters** or anyone who looks like they should not be in your neighborhood. Natural disasters can often bring out people who are looking for easy opportunities to rob and steal, so make sure you're ready to defend your home and your family.
- **Your rights could be stripped quickly.** Depending on the size of the earthquake, and the resulting chaos that follows, the government might restrict personal rights, as we've seen in a number of previous disasters.

WHAT CAN YOU DO TO MINIMIZE THE THREAT?

Because of their unpredictable nature, earthquakes are probably one of the most difficult natural disasters to prepare for. Because there are no effective early warning systems for earthquakes, you need to take the time to understand the dangers and take the proper precautions before a quake hits.

However, there are a number of safety precautions you can take before an earthquake to protect yourself and minimize damages:

- Put together an emergency kit/bug out bag that's filled with the supplies you need to survive an extended disaster. (See chapter five.)
- Firmly secure large appliances, water heaters, heavy objects, mounted televisions, and anything that can fall and cause injury during a quake. Most home improvement stores sell earthquake straps, bolts, and other stabilizing equipment.
- Remove any large items that are near your bed such as mirrors, picture frames, and artwork.
- Install safety latches on cabinets to prevent them from opening during a quake.
- Have an evacuation plan in place that includes a way to contact everyone in your family should the quake hit when you're separated. (See chapter four.)
- Practice your emergency evacuation plan on a regular basis. Everyone in your family should know exactly what to do when disaster strikes.
- Keep your cell phone nearby at all times and make sure it's always fully charged.

STAYING SAFE DURING AN EARTHQUAKE

Knowing what to do and then acting quickly during an earthquake can help prevent injuries and save lives.

- **Immediately find a safe location and take cover.** If possible take cover under a sturdy table, or in the inside corner of the building. Cover the back of your head and your eyes.
- **Stay away from windows, exterior doors, and walls**, and anything that can fall on you such as heavy objects, appliances, lighting fixtures, and large furniture.
- **Stay away from doorways.** Many people advise taking cover inside a doorway; this should only be done if you know the doorway is a sturdy load-bearing doorway. If there's any doubt, stay away from doorways.

Most modern homes have poorly constructed doorways that offer little, if any, actual protection.

- **Stay calm and be aware of what's going on around you.** While most experts advise staying inside until the shaking stops, be on the lookout for signs of an imminent collapse of the building or structure.

HOW TO SURVIVE THE AFTERMATH

After the shaking stops, the threat is far from over; in fact, the potential dangers might be even higher during the immediate aftermath of the quake.

- When the quake stops, take a quick assessment of the area to make sure it's safe to move. After things seem safe, immediately make your way outside of the building.
- Do not reenter your home without making a visual inspection for signs of structural damage.
- Expect aftershocks. While aftershocks are usually weaker than the actual earthquake, structural damage can add up with each aftershock, increasing the risk of collapse.
- Watch for fires or things that can cause fires such as downed power lines and broken gas lines. If you smell gas or hear a hissing noise, stay away from the building and call the local gas company.
- When cleaning up, open all cabinets and doors slowly and watch out for falling objects.
- If you live in a low-lying coastal area, be aware of possible tsunamis. Check your local emergency weather stations for tsunami warnings and evacuate if necessary.

Surviving a Wildfire

Over the last couple decades, wildfires have become a growing problem, especially for people living near wooded areas or remote mountain locations. Wildfires can start for a variety of reasons including people carelessly using fire, lightning strikes that go unnoticed, and, unfortunately, by people looking to create chaos.

The first signs of an approaching wildfire are often the smell of smoke, bizarre animal behavior, and the noise of the approaching blaze. If you live in an area that's prone to wildfires, these are all things you need to be aware of and take notice of.

HOW REAL IS THE THREAT?

In and of themselves, wildfires are not necessarily a bad thing. In fact, they're nature's way of cleansing the system and can actually prevent future fires by burning underbrush and regenerating the forests. The problem comes from man's encroachment into these wilderness areas, and our policy of stopping these fires that, in many cases, should be left alone.

After years of suppressing these fires, many wilderness areas have been left dangerously filled with undergrowth and debris that can cause abnormally powerful fires, which can quickly grow out of control. As these wilderness areas become more developed, the threat is only going to increase.

In the United States alone, wildfires have burned twice as many acres per year as they did forty years ago. As more people move into regions bordering wilderness areas, the threat of wildfires increases exponentially, and so does the threat to life. Once a fire starts in these areas, it is incredibly hard to control.

It's estimated that approximately 90 percent of the wildfires in the United States are caused by man, including both deliberate and accidental fires. The remaining 10 percent are caused by natural phenomena such as lightning strikes and lava runoff.

WHAT CAN YOU DO TO MINIMIZE THE THREAT?

While there are some things you can do on a personal level to prevent wildfires, such as always paying careful attention when using fire and observing and respecting no-burn orders, there's not a whole lot you can do to prevent other people from doing stupid things. So the only way you can truly reduce your personal threat is to be prepared to react at a moment's notice.

That being said, there are some things you can do to help:

- **Always follow safe fire-building practices.** Never underestimate what a fire can do.
- **When building a fire, take a good look at your surroundings**. Make sure you're building the fire away from combustible debris, dry grasses, trees, and bushes. You should always build your fire inside of a fire pit, preferably in an area that's been burnt in the past.
- **Always have a way to put out your fire.** If you're building a fire you should always have a way to extinguish it before you ever attempt to light it.
- **Never leave a fire unattended.** While this may seem like common sense, it's one of the most common ways a fire can grow out of control. If you're going to leave your fire, put it out first.
- **Regularly clean your roof and gutters.** Keeping your roof clean will help prevent your home from catching fire due to blowing embers.
- **Keep your land clean.** You should regularly inspect your land for anything that may be combustible. Remove all dead limbs, brush, and debris from around your home.
- **Have firefighting tools on hand.** A fire extinguisher, water hoses, rakes, an ax, and a chain saw can help you fight small fires and can prevent them from growing out of control.

- **Maintain your water supplies.** In most areas affected by wildfires, water is often hard to come by. If you have the means, maintaining an extra supply of water specifically meant for fire control can help. Small ponds, swimming pools, and cisterns are terrific options.

HOW TO PREPARE FOR A WILDFIRE

If a wildfire is threatening your area, there's really only one option—evacuation. While other types of natural disasters may allow you to hunker down, wildfires should never be taken lightly, and staying to protect your home is probably going to get you killed.

- Have your evacuation plan and bug out bags ready. (See chapter five.)
- Find out what warning systems are in place in your area. If wildfires are in the area, pay attention to warning sirens and keep a close eye on local news reports and listen to local radio for updated emergency information on when to evacuate.

HOW TO SURVIVE DURING A WILDFIRE

Again, a wildfire is nothing to play around with. Once the warnings are sounded, you need to evacuate. Immediately roll up your vehicle's windows, grab a wet cloth to cover your mouth as you leave, and put your evacuation plan into place.

If you're caught out in the wilderness without a clear path out:

- Get low to the ground.
- Look for the closest river or pond and make your way to it.
- Cover your head and clothing with water, and crouch down in the water.
- If you're near a river, follow the river out to safety, making sure to stay wet and low while covering your mouth with a wet cloth to protect your lungs from smoke.

When making your way to safety, keep in mind that the most dangerous place to be during a wildfire is uphill from the flames or downwind.

PART THREE:
Surviving Crime and Violent Situations

The FBI estimates that in the United States, over 1.4 million people are active in more than 33,000 gangs. What was once largely an inner-city problem has now grown out of control and invaded rural areas of the country. But it's not just gangs we have to worry about. Violent crime and criminals are everywhere, making it more important than ever to learn how to protect yourself and your family from the evils that are out there.

This section is designed to give you
- a real-world view of what criminals look for and how to recognize their behaviors.
- detailed instructions and steps to keep yourself, your property and your family safe.
- techniques to use when confronted with a crime or violent attack.

The concepts and strategies presented in this section are not untested theories; they are real-world techniques and advice born out of necessity. They have been tested in real-life situtations against criminals and can be used to protect yourself and your loved ones from this growing threat.

This section is not filled with a bunch of fancy martial arts moves or regurgitated garbage written by someone who has never had to defend himself on the streets; it's filled with invaluable advice that will help you avoid danger, protect your loved ones, and defend yourself when confronted with an imminent attack.

⑫ Situational Awareness and Crime

Most of the information you read about criminals and criminal behavior is put together by college professors or criminal profilers; the problem with that is everything they're telling you is based purely on theory or their academic observations. It's one thing to develop a bunch of theories based on case studies while sitting in the safety and comfort of your office. It's an entirely different thing to learn about crime as you're looking down the barrel of a gun.

So to really understand the criminal mindset, you must go deeper. There are simply some things that can't be learned through reading case studies or studying crime statistics. While the best way to understand the criminal mindset is to talk to the criminals, most of them aren't going to open up and share their secrets. So the next best thing, and where I'm coming from on the issue, is talking to someone who has lived with criminals and has had to learn how to survive in their world. And trust me, their world is not your world, and it's not like anything you've seen in a Hollywood movie.

My observation and my advice comes from years of living around people who engage in crime. I've dealt with many of the topics that I'm going to share with you, so everything you're going to read is largely based on my real-world experience. It's also based on my relationships with some pretty nefarious people—hey, I grew up living in some pretty rough cities. If you didn't associate with some of these people you probably weren't going to survive for very long.

The goal of this chapter is to help you develop a self-defense mindset that will help you avoid being a victim of crime, or if avoidance isn't possible, to survive the situation with as little harm as possible. To really understand self-defense, and to wrap your head around why learning how to protect yourself is so important, we must first look at the criminal mindset.

THE CRIMINAL MINDSET
There are a few characteristics that are found in nearly all criminals.

Criminals Are Very Good at What They Do
While you're hard at work, trying to make a living to feed your family, the criminal is hard at work perfecting his craft. While some of these people aren't the brightest bulbs in the bunch, you have to consider the fact that a criminal has nothing to do all day but think about ways to perfect his skills.

Also remember that many of them have more training and education, in regards to their criminal profession, than most doctors fresh out of medical school. The prison systems are like Ivy League schools for criminals. Twenty-four hours a day, seven days a week these people have nothing to do but learn from other criminals. While I've never been to prison, I grew up knowing a lot of people who have, and I can tell you they come out a hell of a lot smarter and, in most cases, even more ready to get back to their criminal ways.

Criminals Aren't Afraid of Being Caught
Threats of law enforcement do nothing to stop these people. While none of them want to be caught, they aren't scared of the consequences. Like I said, the prison system isn't really a deterrent; in fact, some of criminals look at their time in prison as a mini vacation where they get to perfect their criminal skills.

I haven't been to prison, but I have been to jail a couple of times. I did some dumb things when I was younger that I'm certainly not proud of, but my experiences taught me a lot about real-world defense. I've disclosed this information about my past to tell you what I've seen firsthand, and it sure isn't pretty. Jails are filled with people who have no fear of the prison system. In fact, from what I've seen, most convicted criminals sentenced to a prison term couldn't wait to get transferred from the local jail into the prison system, where, ironically, they have more freedom and more opportunity to perfect their criminal ways.

Criminals Are Selfish

There's only one thing that motivates criminals—they're selfish. Many people in today's society try to excuse criminal behavior by blaming it on things like social injustice, oppression, or economic circumstance. But there is really only one reason for crime: selfishness. Thankfully for the rest of us, selfishness is a weakness that makes the criminal somewhat predictable, and in a way easy to outsmart.

Criminals Plan and Prepare for Their Crimes

This is probably one of the most important things to remember, and has the largest impact on your ability to defend yourself. In the case of a violent attacker, you must understand that the attacker is coming prepared for violence. Not only is he ready to harm you, but he has mentally accepted the fact that he may be harmed in the process. This puts him at a huge advantage.

It's impossible to be instantaneously mentally prepared for a surprise attack, unless you are living in the state of constant paranoia, which I don't recommend to anyone. The criminal, however, is coming to the situation mentally prepared to be harmed, and this is where most wars are won. The guy who's willing to die definitely has the upper hand because there's nothing holding him back.

EVERYDAY SITUATIONAL AWARENESS

Situational awareness is being aware of your surroundings and the potential threats around you. It's a critical skill that you need to develop. Chapter one helped you identify the potential threats around you. In terms of everyday situational awareness—taking notice of what is happening around you in the moment—most people are simply tuned out.

Between texting, daydreaming, or dealing with the never-ending bombardment of modern-day life, most people are tuned into everything except what's really taking place around them. How many times have you arrived at your destination only to realize you have no memory of the route you took to get there? This would be the opposite of situational awareness, and people who live in this state are much more likely to fall victim to criminals, threats, and accidents that could have been easily avoided had they been aware of their surroundings.

Having spent years needing to protect myself on the streets, I can tell you from firsthand experience that situational awareness is the number-one thing you can do to protect yourself. Remember, criminals are coming into the crime or attack with the upper hand. They had the luxury of planning, watching, and waiting for the perfect target. After they've selected you, your best weapon is your ability to spot the danger before it's too late. That being said, if they have selected you, nine times out of ten it's because they picked up on your lack of awareness.

Developing an Everyday Situational Awareness Mindset

There are a number of simple steps you can take to improve your situational awareness. Develop your situational awareness mindset by doing the following:

Identify Threats. The simple act of taking the time to identify the most likely threats you'll face and studying these threats gives you an edge that can help make you a less-appealing target to criminals.

People who go through life in denial about crime often make the best targets; criminals can smell these people from a mile away. Being ignorant of the threats that are out there makes your chances of recognizing and avoiding those threats nearly impossible.

Take control of your personal safety and security. Those who are able to defend themselves because they took the time to train in self-defense are much more likely to spot a potential threat before someone who failed to take the adequate training. Chapter thirteen details self-defense training and practices.

Recognize behavioral clues. Noticing the behavior of those around you is one of the best was to predict an attack. Be on guard and pay particular attention to the action of someone who

- looks noticeably agitated
- looks out of place
- seems to be sweating for no apparent reason
- is overly dressed for the environment
- just seems a little off

Use profiling to your advantage. While this may not be politically correct to say, the fact is criminals often fit certain profiles. The chances of being robbed by an elderly lady in a wheelchair are a lot less likely than being robbed by a teenager who is sporting gang colors and covered in gang tattoos. In my opinion, profiling has nothing to do with race, but does have everything to do with appearance.

That being said, remember that appearances can be deceiving. Smarter criminals are going to try to blend into their environment and will often change their appearance to try to deceive potential victims.

Use technology to your advantage. You can increase your overall awareness by using technology to give you a better idea of what's going on around you. Before going to a large public event, or visiting a large public place like a mall or theater, take a couple of minutes to do some reconnaissance online. Images from Google Earth can give you a good idea of possible escape routes should something happen, and social media websites like Twitter and Facebook can help inform you of disturbances or large-scale acts of violence before they happen. It's kind of shocking, but many of today's violent attacks, riots, and large-scale disturbances are often preplanned and coordinated via social media.

While the thought of people actually bragging about their crimes might be disturbing, it does help give you an extra layer of protection by allowing you to look up your destination before leaving the house. Searching for the name of your destination on a site like Twitter can help you get a better picture of what's going on and can help you avoid potential threats.

Trust your gut. One of the best things you can do is to learn to trust your gut. Our subconscious minds have a way of picking up on subtle details that we might otherwise miss. These small clues often give us a gut feeling that something just isn't right. Unfortunately most people ignore these feelings, and often find themselves in trouble because of it.

Self-Defense for the Real World

Taking control of your personal safety and security is the best self-reliance strategy you can follow to avoid becoming a victim of crime or a violent attack. Self-defense training helps you identify potential threats to your personal safety. Any threat that can be identified can be avoided. This chapter will help you take responsibility for your own self defense.

CHOOSING A QUALIFIED SELF-DEFENSE SCHOOL

When it comes to being able to defend yourself, one of the best things you can do is to find a self-defense school with a qualified instructor who can teach you the skills you need to survive in a variety of attack situations. However, if you're just getting started in the world of self-defense, finding the right school, style, and instructor can be difficult. Locating a martial arts school really isn't the problem, these days there's one on almost every block. The problem is finding an instructor who understands real-world self defense. Remember, your goal is stop an attacker, not to learn a bunch of fancy martial arts moves and forms.

So what can you do? Well, you're going to have to do some research. To start your search, ask a police officer which school he or she would recommend. Police training is all about how to deal with people who have the potential to attack, so their training is usually focused on practical defensive skills that are meant to immediately neutralize the attacker. Chances are a cop will be able to point you in the right direction of a good instructor.

Here are some key questions to ask of any self-defense school you consider:

1. **Does the school offer a trial period?** If the school tries to pressure you into signing a contract the second you walk in the door, chances are

they're only out for one thing—your money. Use the trial periods to test out multiple schools until you find one that feels like a good fit.

2. **What is the primary focus of the school**—teaching forms and maneuvers or offering hands-on self-defense training? Your best bet is to find a school that focuses most of its time on hands-on training and real-world sparring drills.

3. **Does the instructor teach ground fighting?** A majority of fights end up on the ground and any school that ignores that fact, or claims you'll never be knocked down if you learn their style, is not giving you accurate information. Avoid that school at all costs.

4. **Does the school introduce elements of psychological stress?** Fights are fearful situations, so a good school should include aspects that simulate a fear response during the training process.

SELF-DEFENSE MISCONCEPTIONS

As you research schools and instructors, you'll hear a lot of different self-defense terms thrown around. To help you make the best decisions regarding your instruction, I'm going to address some common self-defense misconceptions.

Misconception: Mixed Martial Arts (MMA) training prepares you for real-world self defense.

Reality: MMA fighting is not real-world self-defense. Anyone who wants to argue that point has probably never been in a real-world fight. Yes, some MMA techniques might overlap, but the two styles of fighting are radically different for two main reasons.

First, while MMA might be a little closer to the real world than tournament sparring, it's still a very controlled fight with rules governing what you can and can't do. The last time I checked, no one was entering the ring with the mindset of murdering his opponent. Second, what might work in an MMA fight probably won't translate to the streets. In real life there are no rules; the last thing you want to do when being violently attacked is stay in place and trade blows or, even worse, end up on the ground.

Misconception: Street fighting schools offer real-world fighting experience.

Reality: Be wary of any school that promotes itself as an extreme street-fighting school. In most cases, these schools are filled with guys more interested in looking tough than knowing how to immediately stop an attack. Remember, a real-life attack is not a situation that you want to remain in and trade blows. If that's what the school is teaching, it's not teaching you to defend yourself.

Misconception: A black belt will increase your survival skills and the ability to defend yourself

Reality: Black belts have very little to do with your ability to defend yourself. I have nothing against martial arts as a sport; in fact, I myself have been involved in the sporting side of martial arts since I was a kid. I also enrolled my daughter in tae kwon do when she was five because I think it's a good way to introduce self-defense skills to a child. It also helps with self-confidence, which is a key part of staying safe. That being said, tournament fighting does nothing to prepare you for a real-life attack. I've been in street fights, and I've fought in tournaments—they are two entirely different beasts.

If your goal is learning how to defend yourself, look for a school whose main goal is teaching real-life self-defense skills, not handing out colored belts.

Misconception: Real-life fights look just like Hollywood movie fights.

Reality: Martial arts films don't depict anything close to reality. I'm a huge Bruce Lee fan; I've watched his movies more times than I can count, and I read pretty much anything I can find on him. In real life, Lee's actual fighting philosophy and style were completely different from what he portrayed on the screen. While his on-screen fights tended to last for several minutes and were filled with all sorts of spectacular looking kicks and fancy moves, Lee's own style of fighting, which he dubbed "Jeet Kune Do," emphasized minimal movements with maximum effect and extreme speed. His style dealt with the unpredictability of real-life fighting and emphasized the importance of intercepting incoming attacks and ending the fight as soon as possible. Simply put, it taught people to destroy the attacker before the attacker has the time or opportunity to destroy them. This is always the number-one goal when being attacked.

SELF-DEFENSE WEAPONS

When it comes to self-defense, I'm a firm believer in your right to carry a firearm. In my opinion, carrying a firearm levels the playing field and is probably one of the best things you can do to ensure your safety—right behind your situational awareness and self-defense training.

A firearm is always my number-one choice when it comes to choosing a defensive weapon. That being said, carrying one is becoming a legal nightmare that requires an in-depth knowledge of local, federal, and even international laws. From cities implementing gun-free zones (which should always be avoided at all costs) to the federal government's never-ending assault on the second amendment, the list of places where you can legally carry a firearm is dwindling by the day.

Always Carry Something

I don't know about you but to me, the thought of leaving the house without carrying a defensive weapon is starting to seem more and more like a game of Russian roulette. If you are heading into an area where carrying a firearm is not an option, I recommend finding a legal alternative that can be used as an extra layer of protection.

From Tasers and pepper spray to tactical pens and walking sticks, there are legal weapons you can carry that will make an attacker sorry he ever met you. The main idea when choosing one of these weapons is to find something that you can comfortably carry with you at all times that can be used in conjunction with your self-defense training. A weapon by itself is not enough. You also must have self-defense knowledge and training. Some alternative weapons that can be carried just about anywhere are

- **Kubatons.** A kubaton is a small, close-quarter self-defense weapon that is used to attack soft tissue, bony material, and nerve points. Essentially, it is a small rod, about the size of a marker. And many have a key ring attached to one end so it can be used as a key chain. Many law enforcement officers carry one that can be used with pain compliance techniques. Because a kubaton is basically just a small rod, most places should allow you to legally carry one.

- **Tactical pens.** This isn't your typical ballpoint pen. A tactical pen is typically made from a heavy-duty metal material molded to fit perfectly in your hand. It's used in the same way as a traditional kubaton, but because these pens are fully functioning writing instruments they can be carried in places where your kubaton might raise alarm bells.
- **Walking sticks.** Who's going to tell someone they can't carry a walking stick? Ah, officer, my aching back! Walking sticks make great self-defense weapons because they can be carried just about anywhere in the world, including airports and other places where you could be vulnerable to an attack. They give you the added benefit of being able to fight back from a safe distance.

JUSTIFYING SELF-DEFENSE

If you are forced to use self-defense techniques against an attacker, understand that you may have to defend your actions. If you're smart, you hopefully took every chance you had to escape and avoid as much physical contact as possible. In a self-defense situation, especially one where you severely injure or kill your attacker, there is a good chance you may be arrested. If this happens, you had better be able to show that you had no other options.

Unfortunately, we live in a society that gives criminals far too many rights. For instance, the moment someone breaks into your home, I believe that person has shown deadly intent; sadly, a lot of politicians don't always agree with that assessment. In some areas of the country, people have actually been prosecuted for firing first and asking questions later. Be aware that you are going to have to defend your actions, so make sure you know they are justified.

SAFETY PRINCIPLES FOR CHILDREN

It's sad that we have to teach our kids about the evils of the world. But ignoring the reality of the situation and pretending that these evils don't exist does nothing to prepare your child to face the countless number of very real threats that are out there.

It's your duty as a parent to train your kids how to deal with threatening situations. If you don't teach them differently, most children will blindly obey adults even in the face of immediate danger.

It's OK Not to Be Nice

We all want nice kids, but some parents make the mistake of overdoing it to the point that some kids are physically afraid to say no to an adult. Some adults are afraid to say no, so it's really not surprising that we have so many weak children in this country. You must make sure your children know that they have the power to say no, especially if they feel scared, threatened, or as if they are in danger.

Not All Adults Are Authority Figures

Some kids, unless told otherwise, will automatically see every adult as an authority figure. That's why it's extremely important to teach them that they don't have to obey adults who are asking them to do something that doesn't seem right.

- Let them know that they should never obey an adult who asks them to do something that makes them feel uncomfortable.
- They should know that a normal adult is not going to ask a child for help. Let them know not to approach any adult who is trying to start a conversation with them.
- Make sure you impress the fact that being bigger does not mean someone has authority.

It's OK to Fight Back

It's extremely important to let your children know that they have the right to hurt anyone who is trying to harm them. Our public school systems, in a misguided attempt to stop bullying, continually drill the "it's never alright to put your hands on someone else" message into every student's head.

While children should be taught that fighting is always a last resort, they should never be taught to sit there and take it. If someone is causing them physical pain or attempting to hurt them, there is always a legitimate reason to fight back. I suggest letting them know they have your approval if they have no other option, and that you will always fight to support them.

Fight Like an Animal

I'm sure at some point you've probably witnessed your child have a total meltdown. I'm sure you know exactly what I'm talking about: the kind of meltdown where every eye in the store turns toward you because your child is shrieking at the top of his lungs, flailing around like a crazed lunatic.

While this behavior is less than desirable in a store full of people, this is exactly what your child should be taught to do when confronted by an adult attacker. The more attention your child draws to his situation, the more likely he is to come out unharmed. Teach your child to

- Respond like a crazed animal. He should be kicking, screaming, and yelling things like "STRANGER," "CALL 911," "HELP".
- Bite. Scratch. Stick her fingers in the attacker's eyes and do anything she can to escape.
- Use pencils, keys, or anything he carries with him as a weapon. Show him how to jam these things into the throat, the eyes, and any other vulnerable areas of the body.

Don't Just Talk to Them, Show Them

One of the most effective ways to teach your children the skills they need to stay safe is to role-play a variety of dangerous situations with them. You don't have to give them the reasons people do bad things, but you should let them know what situations are right, what things are wrong, and how to react to them. By role-playing a variety of situations, you will help them instinctively act without anxiety if they're ever put in a dangerous situation.

PRACTICE SITUATIONAL AWARENESS

Show your kids what kinds of things to look out for and teach them to notice what people are doing.

- When you're out in public, point things out to them.
- Make it a game. See who can find things like exits in a building or where to run if someone was attacking them.
- Teach them to look for moms with kids, large groups of workers or police and firefighters. These would all be good people to seek out when lost or when being followed by an adult.

Enroll Your Child In a Self-Defense Class

I think every kid should be enrolled in some type of self-defense course. While I advise adults to be a little more selective when looking for an instructor, when it comes to small children most martial arts schools are a good start.

Just make sure the school spends a portion of its time teaching self-defense measures. For adults who don't know what I'm talking about, there's a big difference between martial arts as a sport and the use of martial arts to defend yourself from an attacker.

Home Security and Surviving a Home Invasion

I approach the topic of home security from the point of view that no one can do a better job than you of defending your own home from an attacker. This is especially true during a natural disaster or crisis situation when law enforcement officials will likely be too busy dealing with the aftermath of the event to respond to calls for help.

Even during the best of times, home safety is a major cause for concern. According to FBI statistics, in the United States alone more than 1.5 million homes are burglarized each year. That makes home invasions and burglaries two of the most likely crisis situations you'll face, making it something you can't afford not to prepare for.

Between criminals looking to enrich themselves by stealing your hard-earned valuables to people who have even more sinister motives behind their criminal undertakings, the need to protect your home has never been greater.

When it comes to natural disasters, or in the case of a prolonged economic crisis, the ability to protect yourself, your home, and your family from chaos is important. If you haven't taken steps to secure your home and figured out how you will defend it from intruders, you're doing yourself and your family a huge disservice and putting all your lives in danger.

HOME SECURITY AND DEFENSE DURING A DISASTER

One of your top concerns during any type of disaster is going to be the safety and security of your home and family. All your preparations and planning are going to be useless if some loser decides he's going to kick in your door and take what you have. When disaster strikes, you are your family's 911.

Even during the good times, when everything is relatively calm, most police officers will tell you there's very little they can do to prevent a home invasion or burglary. During a crisis situation, when first responders will be taxed beyond their capabilities, counting on law enforcement to stop a bad guy is even more unrealistic and is not a legitimate plan for survival.

Natural Disaster Security Concerns

- Disasters can bring out the worst in people, and the likelihood of crimes such as home invasions and looting go way up during times of crisis.
- Security features that require electrical power may be compromised during a natural disaster. Emergency lighting, home alarms, and electronic surveillance are going to be useless when the grid goes down.
- You are on your own. During times of crisis, first responders are going to be hard to come by. The chance of being able to call 911 and have the police respond in a timely manner is going to be pretty low.
- You need to learn how to become your own first responder. That means being able to protect your home from criminals and looters.

HOME INVASIONS

- Long before the criminal commits his crime, he has gone through the process of planning and mentally preparing for the criminal act. The moment he enters your home, he is already a step ahead of you because of his planning and mental readiness to do what he needs to do.
- Chances are, the attacker is coming prepared for violence. He understands the risks, has made the mental calculations, and is mentally prepared to take action.
- The criminals who commit these types of crimes have very little to lose and are usually willing to do anything they can to get away with their crime, including taking the life of anyone who gets in their way.
- You must assume that any home intruder is armed and dangerous. If they are crazy enough to break into a home, there's a good chance they are crazy enough to take a life.

FIREARMS FOR HOME DEFENSE

You need to be able to defend your home: that means having a firearm. I've seen some survival books suggest that guns have no place in disaster preparedness. In my opinion, the people who say that are either blinded by political ideology or have no clue about criminal behavior and what it takes to survive in the face of this type of danger.

You can choose to believe whatever you want when it comes to the politics of firearms. But when it comes to criminal behavior and protecting yourself from someone whose sole purpose is to do you harm, the real world starts to take over.

Criminals don't care about gun laws; if they cared about the law, they wouldn't be kicking in your front door to begin with. In most cases, there is no reasoning with someone who is willing to put his own life at risk by breaking into someone else's home. The moment that person enters your home, all bets are off—including your political beliefs.

The simple fact is, when it comes to the safety of your family, their protection needs to be your number-one consideration and the driving motivation behind any good security plan. I can promise you that the criminal has considered his plan, his own safety, and his motivations well in advance of choosing your home. He is likely willing to do whatever it takes to win. Do you really want to gamble with your family's safety by ignoring the cold hard facts of what it truly takes to be secure?

Firearms in the hands of law-abiding citizens can save lives, and the numbers show it. Every year over two million law-abiding citizens draw their firearms in personal defense, saving a countless number of lives and serving as a serious deterrent to criminals. Often, the mere presence of a firearm is enough to stop a criminal dead in his tracks, without ever having to fire a shot.

Firearm Home Defense FAQ

How much ammo do you need? My school of thought is that you can never have enough ammunition. When it comes to defending yourself during a home invasion, I suggest thinking about it from the perspective of how much ammo you can carry in your firearm. That means buying a firearm that offers you the ability to hold as much ammunition as your local laws will allow.

Unfortunately, in some areas the amount of ammunition a gun's magazine can hold is limited. So you will have to balance local laws with the safety of your family. But in general, the more ammunition your firearm holds, the more protection you afford yourself.

Even the best shooters in the world can miss during a stressful home invasion scenario, so don't make the mistake of thinking that because you're great at the range you only need a certain amount of ammunition to stop an intruder. I always fall on the side of being over-prepared, especially in the face of a dangerous home invasion.

What type of gun is best for home defense? This is incredibly difficult to answer. On one hand, stopping power is incredibly important; but in a home defense situation, you also need to consider what lies on the other side of those walls. Most homes are constructed of very thin walls that are not made to stop a bullet.

The moment you fire a gun inside your home, you risk hitting anything that lies on the other side of the wall. So while I fully agree that stopping power is an important factor when choosing a caliber, so is the safety of everyone in and around the house.

My best advice when choosing a gun for home defense is to weigh the options very carefully and spend time shooting with an instructor who is specifically trained in home defense situations. Your comfort, unique needs, and skill level are going to be far more important than the brand or caliber of the firearm.

Do you need a gun safe? While some experts say a gun safe makes it harder to retrieve your gun when you need it, if you have children, not having a gun safe is really not an option.

To give yourself quick access to your firearms during a home invasion, your gun safe should be located in an area where you can quickly access it. Also, for quick access I suggest looking into something with a Simplex locking mechanism. They are simple to use, fast and easy to access, and don't require batteries or keys to operate.

TRAIN FOR DEFENSIVE SITUATIONS

Firing a gun inside a home during a defensive situation is not the same as firing a gun at the range. While range time is important and will help make you a more accurate shooter, you need to find a training facility that specializes in realistic defensive situations.

Which firearm accessories do I need? There are a million and one different add-ons and accessories for most firearms. When it comes to home defense, especially when faced with having to fight off an intruder in a nighttime situation, a good tactical flashlight and laser sight are two accessories that are well worth the money.

A SECURE HOME HAS MULTIPLE LAYERS OF DEFENSE

When starting to lay out a home security plan, your foundation should be built upon adding as many layers of deterrence and defense as you can.

The more obstacles an attacker has to go through, the more likely he is to move on to an easier home. Most criminals are looking for easy targets, so creating these extra layers of defense will at the very least give them a momentary pause, which can give you enough time to detect the threat and put your plans into place.

Defense Layer 1: External Deterrents

The first layer of defense starts outside your home, and it's all about deterrence. If you can stop an attack before it ever happens, you immediately cut off any possibility of harm to yourself and your family. The idea here is to take away the criminal's tactical advantage and to add highly visible security deterrents. External deterrents include:

Visible security measures. Fences, motion detecting lighting, security system signage, security company decals on your windows, and *beware of dog* signs, can all act as deterrents, giving most criminals enough reason to think twice when targeting your home.

Remove the criminal's advantage. Criminals don't like to operate in plain sight and will be looking for external features they can exploit—shrubs near windows that can conceal their attempt to enter, ladders sitting outside your home that can give them access to second-story windows, and things like trees that extend over roofs or toward second-story windows all need to be considered. Survey your property for these things and remove them immediately.

Add hedges or thorny bushes around the perimeter of your land. While bushes near a window can help conceal an intruder, hedges placed around the perimeter of your property can create a funnel that drives the attackers into one area. This can help give you a clear view of what's coming and/ or a clear line of fire in a defensive situation. To get even more bang out of your perimeter defense, consider planting thorny bushes that can be a huge psychological deterrent and help ensure the attackers have only one way in to your property.

Consider buying a guard dog. Unlike electronic security systems, which are vulnerable to power outages, a good guard dog is a natural-born security system. Not only can it alert you to potential intruders, but it can also create enough fear to make most potential intruders think twice about targeting your home. Guard dogs offer an extra layer of security and can be a powerful self-defense weapon should an intruder breach your security.

Defense Layer 2: Fortify Your Home

The second layer of defense involves fortifying your home. Your next line of defense will require you to think like a criminal, looking for points of entry and any weaknesses in your defenses.

Break into your own home. Putting yourself into the criminal's mind can help you expose weaknesses that you may have overlooked while planning. Scope out your own home and see how many ways you can find to break in.

Strengthen all weak points. Reinforce windows, doorways, and all points of entry into your home. Outfit all doors with high-quality deadbolts and strike plates, and place wooden dowels or locking anchors inside your window tracks.

Secure your windows. Windows are one of the easiest points of entry into most homes. To better secure your home, make sure all your windows are fitted with double-paned laminated glass. As an added security measure, you can also apply specialty window films that will make your glass shatterproof.

Defense Layer 3: Security Systems

The third layer of defense should come from your security systems. Whether it's a professional monitoring system or something that just makes a lot of noise when your home has been breached, you need to install some sort of security monitoring system. Not only will the noise be enough to ward off most intruders, but it will give you the time you need to react before an intruder has the chance to get the drop on you.

Breakage alarms. Installing breakage alarms on all your glass windows and doors can stop an intruder in his tracks. These types of alarms detect small vibrations caused by an intruder who is trying to break your windows.

Battery-power alarms. Some intruders may cut power to your home in an attempt to evade security systems, so you need to think about having an alarm system that can run off a backup power system or 12-volt deep cycle battery.

Door-stop alarms. Battery-powered door-stop alarms are a good, inexpensive way to protect your home that will work even if the intruder cuts power to your home. They look like an ordinary door wedge but are designed to emit a high-volume alarm when an intruder attempts to gain access through a doorway. They are portable, which also makes them a great security device for those who stay in hotels while traveling.

Defense Layer 4: Obstruct Movement Within the Home

The fourth layer involves controlling the intruder's movement if he makes it inside the home. This can be done through the placement of furniture or by placing decoy valuables in an area that draws the intruder to it.

The main objective here is to create what's known as a "kill zone," where the intruder puts himself in a position where he's vulnerable to attack. To do this successfully, carefully study the layout of your home, looking for an open area that you can funnel the attackers into, while at the same time finding an area in your home that conceals your body and gives you an open line of fire.

Defense Layer 5: Safe Room

The final layer in your home defense is your safe room. Your safe room should be placed in an area where your family can immediately make their way to the room during an attack. The route to the room should be clear and help conceal family members as they run to the room. The route should be behind barriers that an attacker cannot shoot around. Even better would be a way to funnel the intruder into a vulnerable position while your family makes their getaway.

SAFE ROOMS

Safe rooms are your most important layer of defense, behind your gun! A safe room is a serious structure built within your home that is meant to protect your family from natural disasters, crisis situations, and most importantly home invasions.

While similar to a storm shelter, a safe room's primary strength and purpose is protection from attacks inside the home. The room is meant to make it harder for home invaders to do you harm.

Building a safe room is not a security shortcut. A safe room is only as good as the plans you have put in place to deal with an attack. That means you need to have a plan in place and do routine drills in which every family member practices exactly what they would do during a home invasion or disaster. It also means stocking your room with adequate supplies and having a way to defend it should an intruder breach the room.

A Safe Room Is Not the Same as Sheltering in Place

As I'll discuss in chapter ninteteen, I'm not a huge fan of something called *sheltering in place*. In my opinion, when faced with a psychopath whose sole purpose is to do you harm, this strategy is flawed at best. Recent mass shootings have highlighted the need to be prepared to protect yourself in the face of a new threat—one where the perpetrator is bent on death and destruction.

While building a safe room may sound at odds with my advice on sheltering in place, I see safe rooms as giving you a tactical advantage. Taking refuge inside of a well-constructed safe room is far different from hiding inside of something like a closet, where the walls offer you little protection from incoming bullets.

A properly planned and constructed safe room will funnel an intruder directly into your line of fire and will be built in a way that makes it incredibly difficult to breach the room. A good safe room will allow you to respond to the threat under your own terms.

That being said, if the opportunity to get out of your home presents itself, it might be a much better option, provided you're sure there's nobody waiting right outside your home.

Key Features of a Safe Room

It needs to be built for defense. When you're designing a safe room, defense needs to be one of the primary considerations during the building process. Your shelter needs to be set up in a way that creates a choke point that allows you to defend yourself from all incoming attacks. If your safe room ends up being a glorified hiding place, you have done little to actually protect yourself from a determined psychopath.

Construction materials need to stop an incoming attack. If you're going to build a safe room, it needs to be done right; that means using high-quality, impact-resistant materials in the building process. Concrete-reinforced walls, steel doors, and reinforced ceilings are all things that need to be considered during the construction process. Your safe room should be able to protect you from not only extreme weather but incoming gunfire as well.

Keep surveillance in mind. Building a room without the ability to survey what's going on outside the room is a huge mistake. Hidden cameras, peepholes, and listening devices are all things that can be added to the room, allowing you to track the movements of everyone inside the home. Just make sure

PRACTICING A HOME INVASION DRILL

1. **Have a signal.** You should have a predetermined signal that tells everyone in your home to put the plan into place. This can be either your alarm system, someone yelling a predetermined word or phrase, or a loud whistle that everyone in the home can hear.

2. **Have a route.** Everyone in the home should have a predetermined route to the safe room. This is especially important in homes where the rooms are on separate floors. In this case, the oldest child should be in charge of the younger children and should be able to make it to the safe room without a parent's assistance.

3. **Know the room.** Once in the safe room, everyone should be fully aware of what is in the room and what steps need to be taken. Children should be taught to be as quiet as possible while in the safe room, and each of them should be taught to immediately call 911 from the safe room phone.

4. **Know your route out.** Every plan should include a way out of the safe room, should the room become compromised. Pick an assembly point outside the house and make sure it's part of every drill you run.

that all electronic surveillance equipment can be powered from within the room in case of power outages or clever burglars who may cut incoming power lines.

Communication is key. A dedicated phone, cell phone charger, ham or CB radio, and an emergency radio should be stocked and ready to use inside the room. The moment you enter the safe room, someone should be trying to make contact with emergency responders.

Emergency supplies. While most home invasions aren't going to last long enough to warrant using these supplies, your safe room should still be stocked with emergency food, water, and first aid supplies in case you need to use the room during a prolonged natural disaster or crisis situation.

Emergency escape route. In my opinion, every safe room needs to have an emergency escape route built into the room's design. Unless you're building a tomb, you need some way out of the room in case things go really bad.

As an added layer of security, the escape route should be built behind a wall or hardened structure within the safe room, giving you the ability to defend the room if the main door is breached. This will give everyone in your family time to make their way to safety while you hold off the attack.

Avoiding and Surviving a Violent Attack

ALWAYS BE AWARE OF YOUR SURROUNDINGS

Most survivors talk about how fast the attack happened, and while many violent attacks may happen quickly, there are usually things that can be done to help you survive or avoid the attack to begin with. That's why staying on guard and paying attention to your surroundings are such an important part of self-defense. If you can avoid or at least recognize the attack ahead of time, you put yourself in control of the situation.

PRESENT YOURSELF AS A PREDATOR, NOT THE PREY

When criminals select their victims, nine times out of ten they select someone they believe can do them no harm. They are looking for weak and easy targets that can be easily attacked with little harm or injury to themselves. This is why you need to shift your entire mindset and be aware of how you present yourself in public. Believe me, criminals can smell weakness from a mile away. It's not very different from a wild animal that attacks the moment it senses the slightest bit of weakness from its prey. On the flip side, if that animal sees you as a predator, it's going to think twice about attacking.

ALWAYS ASSUME THE ATTACKER IS ARMED

Even if you don't see a weapon, always assume your attacker is armed. If someone is crazy enough to attack, you must assume he or she is crazy enough to pull a weapon. Carrying a concealed firearm can definitely level the playing field, so you need to decide ahead of time if that's something you are willing to do.

YOU CANNOT COUNT ON ANYONE TO HELP YOU

Far too many people freeze up when they are violently attacked. Some do so out of fear, others out of the misguided belief that someone will step in and help them. It only takes seconds to be fatally wounded during an attack, so you can't count on police, or anyone else, to be close enough to stop the attacker.

YOU CAN'T TALK THE ATTACKER OUT OF ATTACKING

If someone is in the process of attacking you, the time for trying to defuse the situation with words has ended. Although this might sound like common sense, in the moment, many people make the mistake of thinking they can still convince the attacker to stop. This is a huge mistake. You must realize that in most cases, a violent attacker cannot be reasoned with. Perpetrators don't care about laws, and they probably lack the moral compass to be affected by anything you say. The attacker doesn't need any justification to carry out the attack, and therefore you need to stop trying to reason with the attacker and fight back.

FORGET EVERYTHING YOU THINK YOU KNOW ABOUT FIGHTING

While there are a number of things you can do to avoid an attack, the actual attack is going to be anything but predictable. People make the mistake of thinking a fight is supposed to follow a set pattern, probably because they watched one too many Hollywood martial arts movies and have never been in a real fight. In reality, no two fights are ever the same; most violent attacks are very fluid events that rarely follow a set pattern.

END THE FIGHT AS FAST AS POSSIBLE

Another misconception, again largely fueled by Hollywood movies, is that fights are an exchange of kicks, punches, and self-defense maneuvers. In a real-life fight, if you stand there and try to trade blows you're going to be injured, maybe killed. Your number-one goal is to end the fight as quickly as possible, to limit the amount of damage the attacker can cause. The longer you allow the fight to drag on, the greater harm you put yourself in.

FIGHT DIRTY

In a life-or-death situation there is no such thing as a "dirty fight." This isn't a time to worry about honor, or what people are going to think about you. It's time to think about your life, and you need to do everything in your power to defend it—including things that might be considered "dirty fighting." If you don't have a gun, you need to attack with viciousness and with one goal in mind: destroying your attacker by any means necessary. Kick below the belt. Bite. Scratch and gouge. Pull hair. Whatever it takes to survive.

LET YOUR FEAR DRIVE YOUR COUNTERATTACK

You must fight back. A big mistake that people often make when attacked is to cover their face and take the blows. They go into survival mode. While this might sound like a good thing, it's the exact opposite of what you should probably do, and in most cases it will probably get you killed.

People often mistakenly think of fear as a bad thing. If you let fear control and overwhelm you, yes it can be bad, probably fatal. But if you can use that fear to fuel your attack, you have just tapped into your primordial instincts that have been protecting man since the beginning of time.

I'm not going to go too far into the biological effects of fear, but it is important to know we have these feelings for a reason. The fight-or-flight response is a powerful mechanism that our body has to deal with these situations, and you need to harness that temporary rush of adrenaline to fight your attacker with that same fearsome ferocity that fuels his attack.

When someone has chosen you as a victim, he's already decided he can win. He is coming at you with pure aggression. This person has pre-planned the attack inside his head and probably has little to no fear. He has one goal and that is to destroy you. The only real way to fight that kind of naked hostility is to change your mindset and let that moment of fear drive your attack.

Avoiding and Surviving a Sexual Assault

Sexual assaults are like all crimes in the fact that the perpetrator is looking for vulnerable, easy targets. Unfortunately, in order not to offend anyone's moral or political beliefs, much of the information given to young girls these days has become highly sanitized. This, in my opinion, has created an environment where many young girls have become easy targets for the sickos who commit these types of crimes.

While everyone agrees it's far better to avoid a sexual assault than to have to survive one, political correctness seems to have gotten in the way of helping people avoid dangerous situations. Today young women, and even young men to some degree, are told that their actions don't have consequences. Unfortunately, in today's society even mentioning the fact that someone's actions have consequences can sometimes be misunderstood.

In no way would I ever suggest any victim of sexual assault was "asking for it." In my opinion, the people who say those kinds of things are only one step above the scumbags who commit these types of crimes. But ignoring the fact that certain risky behaviors can often make a person much more likely to be attacked would be doing them a huge disservice.

Just like any crime, there are a number of things that can do to prevent an attack, but until people can seriously discuss the reality of the situation many people are going to be needlessly harmed because of political correctness.

This section will focus on how you can limit your risk and avoid being attacked, as well as offer instructions on how to fight off an attack.

The decisions you make about where you go, what you do, and who you are with greatly determine your likelihood of being assaulted. Avoiding any type of crime, including sexual assault, means you have to be smart, alert, and aware at all times. Remember, criminals don't care about political correctness; they care about finding easy targets. There are things you can do to prevent becoming another statistic.

AVOID DANGEROUS HIGH-RISK SITUATIONS
Be Smart About Being Alone
Even women who take precautions against the most common types of sexual assault, which are assaults committed by someone the victim knows, can still find themselves in a vulnerable situation. Be smart about what you're doing and stay aware of your surroundings, especially when you're alone in public.

- Be aware of your surroundings and know when to trust your gut.
- If you feel uncomfortable, don't be afraid to ask for help. Most stores, businesses, and college campuses have security guards who can escort you to your vehicle.
- Carrying a concealed firearm can level the playing field. I advise finding a qualified instructor who can teach you how to use one and can show you how to fight back during an attack.
- Study the chapters on situational awareness (chapter twelve) and surviving a violent attack (chapter fifteen). The advice in those chapters will help protect you from sexual assaults as well.

Be Smart During Nights Out
Any party scene with excessive drinking is a high-risk situation for sexual assault. Sexual predators know when women are in a vulnerable position and will take advantage of situations where their guard may be down because of drinking or other risky behaviors.

College campuses, nightclubs and bars, house parties, and any event where people are engaging in risky behaviors are all places where you need to be on guard. While these locations aren't dangerous in and of themselves, the behavior that takes place there—especially drinking to the point of blacking out—puts you at risk. While I advise staying away from these types of parties where the main purpose seems to be binge drinking and sex, if you do decide to go out, be smart about how you party.

- Set limits on the amount of alcohol you consume. You probably already know how many drinks it takes to get you drunk. Keep that number in mind when you go out and stay well below it so you are fully in control of your thoughts and actions at all times.
- Always have a designated sober person with you who can be the eyes and ears of your group. In a fog of alcohol you may not notice the sicko across the room who has been stalking you all night, but a sober friend can keep you safe and stay on the lookout for bad situations.
- Be wary of any situation that involves binge drinking or people who engage in heavy drinking, drug use, and other risky behaviors. Even the friendliest-seeming people can completely change when engaging in heavy drinking or drug use.
- Never leave your beverage unattended or accept any drink from an open container. The "date-rape" drug is a real phenomenon.

BE CAUTIOUS WHEN DATING

Unfortunately, most women are often sexually assaulted by someone they know and trust. This is especially true for people who have just started dating someone new. The excitement of a new relationship can cause you to drop your guard, so be wary of allowing your feelings to get in the way of sound judgment.

- Avoid being alone or secluded at the beginning of any relationship.
- Try to go on double or group dates when getting to know someone.
- Don't let your feelings blind you. Listen to friends and family who might be trying to warn you about your relationship.
- Don't ever go to his place or invite him into yours if you live alone. This might sound a little crude, but unless you're planning on having sex there's never a good reason to go to someone's home, especially after a night out. If you don't want to have sex, don't go to his house or bring him into yours simply for your own safety. If it's a new relationship, you

honestly don't know him well enough to guarantee that he will honor your "no" when you are all alone. Don't make yourself vulnerable.

DON'T LET ANGER CAUSE YOU TO DROP YOUR GUARD

All too often people make the mistake of confronting someone who has been making inappropriate comments, sexual advances, or exhibiting crude behaviors. Many women feel empowered by confronting this type of behavior, but this is a huge mistake that can escalate the situation and cause an already unstable person to do something violent. Never confront someone who has acted inappropriately without having others around. You're not going to teach any lessons by being angry and confrontational about the behavior. If someone's exhibiting behavior that you consider threatening, stay as far away as possible and report the person to the appropriate authorities (school administrators, your HR department, law enforcement, etc.)

PROTECTING YOURSELF WHEN CONFRONTED WITH AN ATTACK

Even those who take every possible precaution can still find themselves in harm's way. No matter what we do, there are still going to be sick people in this world that cannot be stopped by changing our behaviors.

If you find yourself in a situation where someone is physically threatening you, now is not the time to play nice. Be sure to follow the instructions throughout part three of this book to give yourself as many advantages as possible when faced with a threat.

Keep these principles in mind:

- Remember your first objective is trying to escape the situation; if you're unable to do that, you are going to have to fight.
- In a life-or-death situation, all rules go out the window. Use everything at your disposal to stop your attacker. Eye gouging, biting, and groin attacks are all fair game when trying to defend your life.
- If you have a weapon, use it; if not, use anything within your reach against the attacker. Just remember every move you make should be

done with as much force as you can muster, and with the thought that your life depends on how hard you fight back.

- Don't stop until the attacker is incapacitated or you have made your escape.

Avoiding and Surviving a Carjacking

Carjacking is a crime of opportunity, and one that has become increasingly popular throughout the world. With the advent of better electronic car security systems, anti-theft devices, and computerized ignition systems, it's become much harder for the average criminal to steal vehicles using traditional methods. Because of this, many unskilled criminals see carjacking as a quicker and easier way to take someone's vehicle.

Over the last couple of years, law enforcement agencies have seen a resurgence in the number of carjackings. Unfortunately they have also seen a trend in which carjackings have become more violent. They are often committed by well-armed criminals who are more than willing to use force to obtain the vehicle.

HOW TO AVOID BEING CARJACKED

The first step in avoiding any attack is to pay attention to what's going on around you, especially if you're traveling through a high-crime area. Public parking lots are one of the top places a carjacker likes to target, followed by city streets, residential driveways or gated entrances, and gas stations.

While Parked or Parking

Because criminals look for easy targets, you are usually most vulnerable when parking or while entering your vehicle. This is often the time when carjackers like to strike.

No matter how big of a hurry you're in, take the time to scan your surroundings before exiting or walking to your vehicle. Watch for anyone who's lurking near or moving toward your parked vehicle.

When pulling into a public parking lot, especially one you may be unfamiliar with, take a minute to drive around the lot before choosing a space. This will allow you to get a feel for the area and give you time to find the safest spot. Always look for well-lit areas, preferably as close as possible to the entrance.

Avoid parking near

- heavily wooded areas
- large vans or trucks
- anything that limits your field of view

When you park your car, leave all doors locked until you are ready to step out of the vehicle. New cars have a few different settings for the automatic door locking option. Often the factory default setting is to unlock the doors as soon as the car is turned off. Be sure to update the setting so doors remain locked until you open the door handle. Also update the remote unlocking option so only the driver's side door unlocks on the first push of the button. The other doors can be unlocked with a second push of the button.

Before you open your door to exit your car, scan the area all around you, including behind you.

While Driving

When driving, there are a couple of things you should do to prevent becoming a carjacking victim:

- Keep your doors locked and your windows rolled up at all times. It's much harder for a criminal to take you by surprise if he has no way of quickly getting to you.
- If someone approaches your vehicle, carefully drive away. If you are stopped at a light and you are in imminent danger, now is not the time to worry about traffic laws. As safely as possible, remove yourself from that situation, even if it means running a red light.
- Driving inside a center lane makes it harder for a would-be carjacker to approach your vehicle.
- If you're driving somewhere and notice a vehicle following you, do not stop. Drive around the block until you're sure you're not being followed.

If the person continues to follow you, call the police and head toward the nearest police station or brightly lit public area.

- If another vehicle bumps your car, you need to be on alert. Carjackers often use this tactic to trick someone into getting out of their vehicle. Roll up your windows, lock your doors, and signal the other driver to follow you. Then call your local police department and drive to the nearest police or fire station.
- Always have an escape route. That means making sure you never get boxed in, and never allow yourself to be put in a situation where you have no options.
- Stay especially alert when pulling up to residential driveways, gates, traffic jams, or any situation that forces you to stop your vehicle.
- When coming to a stop, leave enough room between you and the car in front of you so you can easily maneuver away and around if necessary.
- While stopped, make sure to scan the area, using your mirrors to keep a close eye on what's going on around you.

SURVIVAL DURING A CARJACKING

If you find yourself in a situation where you're being carjacked:

Get out of the car as fast as you can.

If you find yourself in a situation where a carjacker has entered your vehicle, your number-one priority is to escape. I don't care how much you love your car; no vehicle is worth losing your life. If a carjacker tries to force you to go with him, your best chance of survival is to refuse, fight back, and do everything you can to escape. Your chances of survival go down the second you allow yourself to become captive.

Throw your keys, then run in the opposite direction.

Be alert to where you throw your keys. Identify the safest place to run and throw the keys in the opposite direction so you are running to safety and not further isolating yourself. If the carjacker is interested in stealing your car, he's going to

WHAT A CARJACKER LOOKS FOR IN A VICTIM...

- Easy targets who are not paying attention to their surroundings
- People who have their windows rolled down while stopped at intersections controlled by stoplights or signs
- Anyone talking on a cell phone while parking in public lots and garages
- People using drive-up ATMs
- People who leave their vehicles open and or running at gas stations, car washes, or in their driveways in the morning

go after the keys, allowing you to put distance between yourself and the attacker. If he starts to follow you, you immediately know what the attacker is really after, and you should be prepared to protect yourself if you are caught. Don't stop to fight. Outrun the criminal if possible.

Staying Safe While Using Public Transportation

(18)

At some point, especially if you routinely travel, using public transportation will probably become inevitable. From public trains and buses to taxicabs and other modes of public transport, you need to protect yourself from the dangers associated with this form of transportation.

Traveling on any type public transportation can be risky, especially if you are unfamiliar with the area, traveling alone, or traveling through dangerous neighborhoods. Staying alert while traveling on buses, trains, subways, and inside taxicabs is one of the best things you can do to reduce your risk of becoming injured or becoming a victim of theft or assault.

GENERAL TRAVEL SAFETY GUIDELINES

- **Always stay on guard.** Watch your surroundings and the people around you, and be wary of anything that looks out of the ordinary.
- **Avoid distractions.** Stay off your cell phone, avoid playing with electronic gadgets, and don't wear headphones or listen to music that will limit your ability to hear what's going on around you.
- **Avoid looking like you're carrying valuables.** Keep all valuables out of sight. Avoid playing with expensive smartphones, electronic gadgets, or wearing anything that looks valuable.
- **Always stay awake.** One of the worst things you can do while taking public transportation is allowing yourself to fall asleep. Stay awake; criminals are looking for vulnerable targets and you need to stay on guard.
- **If possible, never travel alone.** One of the best ways to ensure your safety when traveling is to have an extra set of eyes. This not only helps

you keep an eye out for potential problems, but it makes you a less desirable target for criminals who are looking for easy victims.

TRAIN SAFETY TIPS

- When waiting for a train or subway, try to wait in an area that's occupied by other people.
- On the platform, stand well away from the tracks, preferably with a wall behind you.
- Upon entering, immediately make a quick scan of the train. Make a mental note of what kind of people are on the train, where the exits are, and how many seats you are from the exit.
- Try to choose a seat in a car that is either near the train operator or near official personnel.
- Keep a clear view of your surroundings. Avoid choosing seats that obstruct your view of what's going on.
- Try to blend in. Looking like a tourist makes you an immediate target to those looking to take advantage of vulnerable visitors.

BUS SAFETY TIPS

- Know what neighborhoods are on your route before getting on the bus.
- Avoid getting off at isolated bus stops.
- When waiting for the bus, try your best to wait in well-lit areas occupied by other people.
- One of the best places you can sit is near an exit, preferably near the driver.
- Stay awake; criminals are looking for vulnerable targets and you need to stay on guard.

TAXI SAFETY TIPS

- Make sure it's a real taxi. Take a careful look for the taxi's licensing documents, the official markings, and make sure the company is legitimate.
- Ask for driver ID before getting into the cab.

- Avoid being too flashy. Even in a taxi, you should avoid taking out any valuables or looking like you have a lot of money.
- Confirm where you are going. Before stepping foot inside the taxi, make sure the driver knows where you need him to go and confirm the route.
- When traveling alone, sit directly behind the driver. This will give you a good view of what he's doing through the rearview mirror while at the same time limiting his view of you.

TRAVELING WITH FIREARMS

I am a big proponent of always traveling with your firearm; if you carry one back at home, there's no reason not to carry one while traveling. I would argue you probably have more of a reason to carry.

That being said, lawmakers are making it more difficult by the day for law-abiding citizens to exercise their right to defend themselves. So before taking anything that can be considered a weapon, including firearms, knives, and even things like pepper spray, you need to thoroughly study the local laws of anywhere you'll be traveling.

Know Your Rights

The U.S. Department of Justice issued a written opinion that people who travel on airlines with guns are protected under the "Safe Passage" provision in the Firearm Owners' Protection Act. This means that if you follow their regulations, you should be able to bring your guns with you on most trips inside the United States.

Check-in Only

Attempting to bring a firearm, ammunition, or any other weapon on a plane in your carry-on luggage or on your person can and will land you right in jail. You must check all firearms.

The regulations have a number of stipulations that you should be aware of:

- You must be traveling to and from a location in which you may legally have a firearm.

- When driving to the airport your firearm must be unloaded and unreachable from the passenger section of the vehicle.
- The firearm must be transported directly to the check-in desk unloaded and in a locked hard-sided container. (Your case must be completely secure and should not be able to be pulled open when locked.)
- Guns need to be declared at check-in.
- The person transporting the firearm needs to go directly from his vehicle to the check-in desk.
- Ammunition must be secured in a fiber (cardboard), wood, or metal box specifically designed to carry ammunition.
- Keep in mind that some airlines have their own rules and regulations concerning traveling with firearms. It's always a good idea to ask the airline for their policy before planning your trip.

I should also point out that because gun laws are constantly changing and can vary from state to state, double check with the TSA and local law enforcement in any area you plan on traveling. Not checking the local gun laws has landed a number of people in jail who are now facing serious time in prison, so please don't take the need to do your own checking lightly.

LIMIT WHAT YOU CARRY

I'm all for someone's right to defend himself, but I also want to limit the amount of TSA scrutiniy and hassle while I'm traveling. The last thing I want to do is be held up by some overzealous agent who has a problem with the second amendment. In most cases, I try to limit the amount and type of weapons I bring. I also try to avoid bringing anything that might look intimidating, or tactical, which will draw extra scrutiny from inpsection agents.

Surviving an Active Shooter Situation

(19)

It seems like every time you turn on the news, there's another story about some disturbed person killing and terrorizing a bunch of innocent people in broad daylight in a public place. What was once an almost unthinkable and unimaginable event has sadly become so commonplace in today's world that many of these stories don't even make the headlines on the evening news anymore. The active shooter phenomenon is something that you have to be aware of, and at the very least recognize as a possible threat.

WHAT YOU NEED TO KNOW ABOUT ACTIVE SHOOTER SITUATIONS

These events are often performed by a lone gunman, many of whom are either suffering from mental illness or have been taking prescription medications that have altered their mental abilities. In most cases, their sole purpose is to kill as many people as possible.

Some important things to keep in mind about people who commit mass shootings:

- The shooter is usually hell-bent on inflicting mass casualties and generally cannot be reasoned with.
- The shooter typically commits suicide after the event, so he's not scared of dying. If you're in a situation where you have to defend yourself, remember to make it count because the mere threat of confrontation probably won't stop the shooter from finishing his mission.
- The shooter typically has multiple weapons, large amounts of ammunition, and may show up wearing full body armor.

AREAS AND ACTIVITIES AT HIGH RISK FOR SHOOTINGS

Avoid Gun-Free Zones

While this may seem counterintuitive, especially to those who believe banning guns is going to solve the world's problems, the fact is, most mass shooting events happen in gun-free zones.

The madmen who commit these crimes want to kill as many people as possible, so they often choose areas where they know people will be unarmed and unable to stop their attack.

Avoid High-Profile Events

We live in a media-driven society where everybody is looking for their fifteen minutes of fame. Unfortunately when it comes to the psychos who commit mass shootings, this means more often than not they will choose a place that guarantees sensationalized coverage.

- Avoid opening night events.
- Avoid sold-out shows and concerts.
- Avoid high-profile events and politically charged rallies.

Avoid Being an Easy Target

If you do go to a large event such as a movie, concert, or rally, there are a couple things you should do to avoid being an easy target:

- Choose seats that give you a good view of what's going on around you.

SHELTERING IN PLACE

In my opinion, sheltering in place is almost never an option. Hiding and hoping the police will come to your rescue is not your best option—getting out of the area is. By the time anyone is able to respond to the situation, there is a good chance you'll already be dead.

- Situate yourself in a way that allows for a quick, unobstructed exit.
- Make sure you have multiple ways to get out.
- If possible, try to pick an area where nobody can sit behind you.

PRECAUTIONS TO TAKE TO AVOID AN ACTIVE SHOOTER SITUATION

We can't predict when and where these types of shootings will take place, so it's important to be prepared. Here are steps you can take to protect yourself from these types of events.

Pay Attention to Your Surroundings

Being able to protect yourself in an active shooter situation begins with having a good sense of what's going on around you.

- Limit your use of cell phones, headphones, or any other electronic device in public that pulls your attention away from your surroundings.
- Before entering any public place, make sure you get a good feel for your environment. Scan the area, looking for anyone who looks out of place.
- If anything looks out of place, or your gut tells you something isn't right, you need to trust your instincts.

Always Know Your Exit Points

Part of being aware of your environment means knowing how to get out when things go bad. One of the first things I do when entering a building, or any other public place, is to look for every possible escape route and exit. Not only can it help during a shooting, but it's also an important part of being prepared for natural disasters and building fires.

- When entering a building, immediately scan the area, looking for exit signs and doors.
- Continue to make mental notes on the building's layout, and think about how you will reach your exit points should it become necessary.
- Look for alternative exits like windows, emergency doors, and fire escapes.
- Be aware of corners and hallways that can be used as cover while you

are trying to exit the building (turning a corner can help put you out of the shooter's line of fire).

Trust Your Gut

One area of situational awareness that's often ignored is our subconscious ability to pick up on subtle details that may alert us to danger.

In interviews following the 2012 Aurora, Colorado, mass shooting, a number of the survivors admitted they had a bad feeling the moment they saw the shooter enter the building. Even as shots were being fired, a number of people actually stayed in the building, reasoning that the gunfire had to be some sort of promotional stunt related to the movie they were watching.

If a situation seems odd, if something seems out of place, or your gut tells you something bad is about to happen, listen to your instincts and don't wait around to find out what happened.

SURVIVING AN ACTIVE SHOOTER SITUATION

Should the unthinkable happen and you find yourself in the middle of an active shooter situation, there are a couple of things you can do to help maximize your chances of survival.

Do Everything You Can to Safely Exit

During an active shooter situation, the first thing you want to do is remove yourself from the situation. As soon as you hear a shot, or anything that sounds suspicious, immediately start making your way toward an exit point.

- While keeping a close eye on what's going on around you, move as fast as you can toward your exit while trying to maintain some sort of cover.
- If possible, try to turn corners or put yourself behind objects that remove yourself from the shooter's line of fire.
- Once outside the building, stay on guard watching out for other shooters who may be waiting for the exiting crowd. Safely move as far away from the building as possible before calling 911.
- Keep an eye out for police officers, who could mistake you for the

shooter while you are making your exit. Upon exiting the building, stay on guard and be prepared to follow law enforcement instructions.

Take Cover

If you can't safely make it to an exit, the next best option might be to take cover and get ready to respond to the threat. Just remember what makes for good cover in a Hollywood movie sucks in real life. Out of sight does not mean you are out of the line of fire. There's a big difference between taking cover behind a solid barrier like a concrete wall and hiding behind a chair or table.

This is best explained using tactical definitions. From a tactical perspective, *cover* is anything that can actually stop a bullet—a concrete wall, for example. *Concealment* is anything you can hide behind but doesn't stop a bullet. A chair or table or even a wooden or thin metal door are not cover; they are concealment. Concealment objects may offer protection in the movies, but in real life a bullet will rip right through them and right into you. Remember: Out of sight does not mean out of the line of fire.

Taking cover does not mean sheltering in place or hiding from the attacker. When taking cover, never let your guard down. Your mind should always be on either escaping the situation or being ready to fight back.

Fight Back

Critics of this option will probably argue that you should never try to attack a shooter. But if you're in a situation where there's no place to run and no place to seek cover, what other option do you have? Most critics fall silent when asked that question.

The fact is, in an active shooter situation you often have very few options.

- If you have no other options, you need to act quickly and decisively to try to take out the shooter. Hopefully you conceal carry and have the training it takes to respond to this type of situation.
- If you don't have a gun, your best option is probably to rush the shooter when he's switching out ammo magazines.
- If you can't wait, throwing something or shining a bright flashlight into the shooter's eyes can temporarily distract him and give you enough time to act.

Surviving Workplace Violence

According to OSHA, almost two million American workers are assaulted or threatened with violence in the workplace every year. In fact, homicide is now the second leading cause of occupational deaths in the United States.

While the news media generally only reports on sensational mass shootings, the fact is, workplace violence is a huge problem that happens far more often than what gets reported on the evening news.

WARNING SIGNS OF POTENTIAL WORKPLACE VIOLENCE

As with all crimes, situational awareness is the number-one thing you can do to limit the likelihood of becoming a victim. Always be alert to what's going on around you. In the case of workplace violence, there are some warning signs to look out for.

Keep a close eye on anyone who exhibits these early warning signs:
- intimidating or bullying type behavior
- consistently uses verbally abusive language
- changes in a person's typical behavior (becomes more withdrawn, anxious, irritable, etc.)
- increase in the number of arguments with other employees or management
- anyone who either jokingly or seriously verbalizes a desire to harm others

If a coworker exhibits any of these behaviors, make a quick written record of what you witnessed, noting the date and time it took place and who was involved. Then notify your HR department immediately. Your record will help you remember the important details and help you explain your concerns in a concrete way so the company can take necessary steps to fully address the issue.

It's important to be specific and cite examples of the threatening behavior. This will also help protect you from legal action should you have to use any form of self-defense against this person in the future.

WHAT TO DO WHEN CONFRONTED BY VIOLENCE AT WORK
Remove Yourself From the Situation
The best way to prevent becoming a victim is to remove yourself from any situation that seems to be spiraling out of control.

- If someone in your workplace is becoming noticeably agitated, starts screaming at you or anyone else in the area, or starts exhibiting signs that she may become violent, immediately remove yourself from the situation. Confronting the person will likely only make them more agitated and could escalate the situation.
- If someone enters your workplace with a weapon, your first thought should be escape. Immediately get behind cover and move as fast as you can to an exit. Stay low and keep moving—a moving target is harder to hit. Fighting back may seem glamorous in the movies, but in real life it doesn't take much to end your life.
- After you have safely made it outside the building, don't drop your guard. Watch for other shooters who may be waiting to ambush those who are escaping, and then get as far away from the building as possible.
- After you are in a safe location, call 911.

Do All You Can to Get Out of the Building
Many survival experts recommend sheltering in place during a mass shooting event. I believe this advice is no different than telling someone to hide inside their office while the building is on fire—in both cases the advice is not only stupid, it's probably going to get you killed.

In most mass shooting events, the shooters are usually not the greatest marksmen. It's a lot easier for them to hit a stationary target than for them to hit a target that's quickly and stealthily moving away from the situation. Your number-one objective should always be escape.

Develop a Survival Mindset

The most important part of surviving any violent attack is to keep your wits and decide that no matter what happens you will not become a victim. Those who develop a mindset of not giving up and doing everything within their power to live are far more likely to survive. Fear will be a natural reaction to the situation, but don't let it incapacitate you.

Fight Back Only If You Have No Other Choice

If there's no possible way to escape the situation, you're going to need to do everything in your power to fight back. If you have no way to escape, your only option is to fight. In this type of situation, you must be willing to do everything in your power to neutralize the attacker. Review chapter thirteen on self-defense and make sure you are properly trained.

- If your life is being threatened, it's not the time to sit there and trade blows. Your main objective is to end the conflict, which means making sure the attacker is not able to fight back.
- If you are allowed to conceal carry at work, you automatically give yourself an advantage over unarmed coworkers. Just remember that if you do carry a gun, you need to train for these types of real-world scenarios. Shooting at a paper target is one thing, but during life-threatening situations even the best shooters can be affected by stress. Find an instructor who can train you in real-world situations while simulating stressful events.
- If you don't have the option of carrying a firearm, your next best option is to grab anything within your reach that you can use as a weapon. Fire extinguishers, heavy or sharp objects, basically anything that will put a stop to the attack should be used to protect yourself. Your main objective is to end the conflict, which means making sure the attacker is not able to fight back.

Surviving a Hostage Situation

There are three types of hostage takers that the average citizen has to worry about: career criminals, terrorists, and mentally unstable people.

In general, career criminals are the least worrisome because they usually take hostages as a way to get away with their crimes. While these people are still dangerous, their motivations are much different from those of terrorists or mentally disturbed people because their main objective is usually not to kill the hostages. On the other hand, terrorists and mentally unstable hostage takers are a totally different ball game. More often than not these people are intent on taking lives, and this type of hostage situation requires a far different approach.

WHAT TO DO IF YOU'RE TAKEN HOSTAGE

Stay Calm

Your first priority is to try and calm your nerves. While this may sound difficult, your best chance of survival comes from immediately trying to calm your nerves. The best way to do this is dig deep and find your reason to live. Think about your kids, your spouse, or something that you know you have to live for and let that mental image be your driving force. Decide that no matter what happens, you will survive for the sake of whatever your reason for living is.

Be Observant

As you start to calm down, determine what type of situation you're in, and then go into observation mode. Scan the area looking for things like exit points, places to take cover, possible weapons, and anything else you can use to your advantage. At the same time, it's crucial to start paying attention to your captors. Take note of the following:

- How prepared are your captors? Was this a spontaneous thing, or do they seem like they've trained for this event?
- What is their emotional state? Watch for any changes. This is especially important in determining your overall risk of being killed.
- Watch for any weaknesses you might be able to exploit.
- Watch for them to drop their guard. The longer the situation drags on, the more likely they are to drop their guard.
- Watch for any signs that the situation might be turning worse. If you sense they are about to start killing, you have no choice but to take immediate action to fight back.

Make Outside Contact If Possible

If you can make contact with the outside, carefully do it. If you have a cell phone and can get to it without being seen, dial 911 and then hide your phone. Leaving the line open can allow law enforcement to get a better idea of what's going on inside and can help them formulate a plan.

Continually Look for Opportunities to Escape

Some experts recommend hostages give total compliance and wait for the situation to defuse itself. They recommend waiting and letting negotiators do their job. After the September 11th attacks, which made everything ever written about hostage situations obsolete, I think compliance has to be seriously reconsidered.

In today's world, terrorists aren't worried about having their demands met. They likely only have one goal in mind: to kill as many people as possible to support their radical ideology. There is no negotiating with this kind of mindset; they're driven by convictions that cannot be undermined through negotiations. In my opinion, you must always be looking for your opportunity to escape, or if given no other choice, taking the terrorists out.

If Escape Is Not Possible, Attempt to Overtake the Terrorists

When confronted by terrorists, or someone who is mentally unstable, and escape is not possible (for example in the case of a hijacked plane), I think fighting back becomes one of the best options you have. Remain calm and look for your opportunity to take the hostage takers out. In this day and age, I really don't see another option. You either act or you're going to die.

Stay Low and Take Cover When Police Storm In

If police storm in, get down, stay low, and try to take cover. At some point in the hostage situation, where negotiations have broken down or law enforcement believes there is an immediate threat to the hostages' lives, there's a good chance police are going to storm in. When this happens, all hell is going to break loose.

Bullets are going to be flying from every direction, smoke is probably going to fill the air, and in a matter of seconds the chaos will be over. The moment you see the police or hear gunshots, hit the ground. If possible, crawl behind a solid structure like a concrete wall and stay low.

Surviving a Kidnapping

A hostage situation and a kidnapping, while being similar in many ways, usually have very different motivations. When it comes to kidnappings, a kidnapper's motivation is usually either personal in nature—he or she has some sort of infatuation or obsession with the person—or there's motivation by money with the hope someone will pay a ransom for your return.

Remember, most kidnappers are not motivated by killing the abductee. They may be driven by some sick and twisted motives, and they may eventually try to kill the abductee, but killing usually isn't the driving factor. There is actually a good chance the abductee is going to survive the situation if the proper steps are followed.

HOW TO SURVIVE A KIDNAPPING

The first step in preventing a kidnapping is obviously awareness and trying to stop the abduction before it happens. If you can recognize the threat before it happens, or escape the actual abduction attempt, you immediately put an end to the situation.

Fight Back and Refuse to Go

If you find yourself in a situation in which you are being forced into a car or forced to go along with someone, I believe your best bet is to fight back. Do everything you can to resist going with the abductor. Draw as much attention to the situation as you can. Scream, kick, scratch, yell, struggle. Refuse to walk. Make it as difficult as possible for the abductor to move you. If it's only one person attempting to kidnap you, your best bet is probably going to be to immediately fight for your life. Trying to escape before you are taken captive usually outweighs the risks of being injured while fighting back, but you're going to have to determine that based on what's actually going on.

Adapt a Survival Mindset

If you miss your chance to escape while the kidnapping is initally happening, you need to immediately change your mindset. While I believe you should always be looking for a way to escape, now that you've been caught you need to not only calm your own nerves, but you also need to put your abductor's mind at ease. Immediately set your mind on survival, determine that you're going to live no matter what, and start taking actions to control your fear. Don't rock the boat. The sooner the kidnapper stops seeing you as a threat, the sooner he will drop his guard and you can start to again look for the opportunity to escape.

Always Watch for Your Opportunity to Escape

Escape is always your number-one goal, and you should be watching for every opportunity to do just that. Without drawing attention to the fact that you're watching the kidnapper, you should be keeping a close eye on his movements, his mood, his schedule, and anything you can use to help get the upper hand. Unless you are in immediate danger, which would then call for an immediate attack, you should be watching and waiting for the kidnapper to slip up. The second he does, use that opportunity to escape.

Establish Some Type of Rapport With the Kidnapper

If possible, engage the kidnapper in small talk, which does two things. First, it causes the kidnapper to see you as a living person rather than an object. If the kidnapper starts to see you as a person and not an object, he is less likely to harm or kill you. Second, it distracts him and could make him drop his guard, giving you the chance to either attack or make your escape.

One caveat to that would be in the case of someone who's mentally disturbed. Trying to build rapport with someone suffering from a mental illness could easily backfire and cause the person to become even more paranoid.

HOW TO ESCAPE FROM THE TRUNK OF A CAR

Look for a trunk release.

If you're thrown into the trunk of a car, immediately look for the emergency trunk release. A lot of newer cars have a glow-in-the-dark T-shaped handle that will pop the trunk. If you don't see that, feel around for a cable leading to trunk release. Wait for the vehicle to slow down, and then pull the release.

Use the taillights.

If you can't find the trunk release, start pulling back the carpet and look for the taillights. If you can, try to push out the lights so you can stick your hands out to signal for help. If this doesn't work, start yanking out wires. Disconnecting the taillights will hopefully attract police attention.

Look for a tool.

Most trunks will have some type of tools that you might be able to use to your advantage. Search around for the car's tire iron, which can be used to pry open the trunk latch, or to attack the kidnapper the moment he opens the trunk.

Keep Mentally and Physically Fit

If you're in a situation where you have been held captive for a long period of time, you must remember to stay physically and mentally active. The longer you're held in captivity, the more mentally, physically, and emotionally exhausted you're going to become. You cannot afford to give up, and you cannot afford to let your body and mind slip.

- **It's critical to stay mentally sharp.** Do math problems, recall scriptures, write a novel inside your head, and go over escape plans: Do everything you can to stay mentally alert.
- **Find ways to exercise.** Your body needs to be ready to go at a moment's notice, so you need to stay physically fit. This may be hard, but you need to find a way to work out. Do push ups, sit-ups, and any cardio activity you can manage to squeeze in.
- **Set a schedule.** If you can, try to set a schedule. This not only helps you stay sharp but can give you a sense of control that will have a calming effect. Set a time for working out, daydreaming, planning, praying, meditating, and any other small thing you might be allowed to do while being held captive.

Be Careful During Any Rescue Attempt

Rescue attempts can be almost as dangerous as the initial abduction. When police storm in, there is going to be a huge amount of chaos and confusion. Your best bet for surviving the situation is to immediately get down on the ground and avoid any sudden movements.

PART FOUR:
Surviving Man-Made Disasters, Threats, and Terrorism

With the recent nuclear disaster in Japan, numerous economic catastrophes, and an increasing number of terrorist attacks throughout the world, previously unthinkable events have started to become alarmingly commonplace. The way we live, travel, and depend on modern technology has left us incredibly vulnerable to all sorts of manmade disasters and threats. All it takes is one event to disrupt our way of life and cause an unthinkable amount of turmoil.

From nuclear and biochemical terrorist attacks to vital infrastructure shutdowns and cyber-attacks, the world is facing a frightening number of manmade disasters that were once unimaginable. In this section we will look at these threats and discuss detailed survival strategies on how you can keep yourself and your loved ones safe in the face of these 21st century threats.

Surviving a Riot or Flash Mob

Social unrest seems to be at an all-time high, and it doesn't take much for a full-blown riot to erupt. From people rioting after their favorite team wins a sporting event to angry mobs flooding the streets in violent protest over a social injustice, riots are a growing problem that can affect people throughout the world.

Even more troubling is the rise of something called a flash mob; a kind of riot that is actually highly organized and usually preplanned through social media. In recent years, flash mobs have become a growing problem that can quickly overtake entire malls, businesses, or other public venues. If you are unfortunate to be caught in the middle of one of these events, the violence and sheer chaos is enough to intimidate even the most prepared person.

PROTECTING AGAINST THE THREAT OF RIOTS
While riots are extremely dangerous and unpredictable events, there are some things you can do to protect yourself from the threat.

Avoid High-Risk Events
If you're walking along and see a burning building, would your first thought be entering that building? Of course not, but unfortunately many people stupidly put their lives at risk by doing something just as dumb—they attend highly charged events that invite chaos.

- Avoid championship games at any type of sporting event. It's sad but people seem to have a hard time controlling themselves at these types of events; throw a couple of hours of drinking into the mix and it's pretty easy to predict what's going to happen.

PROVING SELF-DEFENSE

While I always say there are no rules in a life-or-death situation, the law might not always have that same opinion. When using deadly force, you had better have a damn good reason to use it because, right or wrong, you are probably going to have to answer to the police.

- Stay away from any type of social justice rally especially if it's a rally to protest a prior act of violence. Ironically, these types of rallies often have a way of inciting even more violence and can quickly get out of control.
- Stay away from large urban centers after any type of political turmoil, election, or large-scale natural disaster.

Follow News Reports and Social Media Activity

If a high-risk activity is taking place in your city, keep an eye on your local headlines and news coverage to keep up-to-date on conditions. You can also get a bird's-eye view of what's really going on by following social media posts made by people at the event. Follow the event's hashtags and set up a Google alert for keywords related to the event. There's probably a good chance, thanks to our fifteen-minutes-of-fame society, that someone is live tweeting what's going on from within the riot.

- If you're concerned about a specific event or meeting, do some online research. Oftentimes people plan their chaos on sites like Facebook and Twitter, which can give you a heads up to what dangers might be waiting for you.
- There are a number of Internet sites and smartphone apps, such as broadcastify.com or Scanner Radio Deluxe for iPhone and iPad, that actually allow you to listen in on local police traffic. This can be a huge

help once the chaos kicks in and can give you valuable information that can keep you safely away from the chaos.

WHAT TO DO IF YOU FIND YOURSELF IN THE MIDDLE OF THE CHAOS

Despite taking all the preparations in the world, you still might find yourself in the middle of one of these chaotic situations. If that happens, remain calm and take the following steps.

Get Away

Your number-one goal is escape. The minute any sort of chaos starts to break out you need to be ready to respond.

- Immediately scan the area for every possible escape route; the second you find one, start to make your way to that exit point.
- If at all possible, try walking with the crowd toward your exit, and never take off running as this will likely draw the crowd's attention right to you.
- Avoid confrontation and try not to attract undue attention.

If You Get Stuck, Blend In

If you were not able to make a quick exit, try to look like you are part of the crowd. Then, as soon as you can safely do so, stealthily start to make your escape.

- Without getting directly involved in the chaos, try to blend into the crowd until you can make a safe retreat.
- If everyone in the crowd is shouting against something, the last thing you want to do is draw attention to the fact that you might have different beliefs. This is not the time to make a point.
- Think of the crowd as a large, raging river. The best way to get out of a river is to swim with the current, and then slowly make your way to the edge. The same is true if you're stuck in the middle of a crowd; the last thing you want to do is go against the current.
- Keep moving with the crowd and do everything you can to stay on your feet. If you fall to the ground, you run the very real risk of being trampled.

Stay Away From Police

While this may sound like an odd piece of advice, especially when your goal is to escape the chaos, during a riot situation there's a pretty good chance the police aren't going to care which side you're on.

Police will likely form a human barricade as an attempt to control the crowd. Officers in riot gear will likely use tear gas, pepper spray, rubber bullets, beanbag rounds, and even high-power water cannons to control the crowd, and they will do so without discrimination. If you're in the middle of the crowd you will be hit.

DEFENDING YOURSELF FROM MULTIPLE ATTACKERS

Due to the highly charged nature of these types of events, there is a very real possibility that you may have to defend yourself from multiple attackers. If you find yourself in a situation where escape or blending in has become impossible and an attack is imminent, your only option is to defend yourself with everything you have inside of you.

If you have a firearm or some sort of weapon, you immediately take away the mob's advantage and give yourself the upper hand. Just remember that you need to act fast, and escape is still your main goal. Your gun only holds a certain amount of ammunition, and once it's gone the crowd is going to come after you very quickly.

If you find yourself in a situation where you have to defend yourself without a weapon, your chances of survival immediately go down. That's why I'm a huge advocate of always being armed. That being said, you should never give up, and you need to do everything within your power to fight to the very end.

- Every counterattack you make needs to count, and it needs to be as devastating as possible.
- Your goal is to incapacitate your attackers, not trade blows. Remember, this isn't a Hollywood movie.
- If you see anything in your immediate vicinity that can be used as a weapon, grab it and use it.

Facing multiple attackers is much different than facing a single attacker. Here are few things to keep in mind if you face an attack by a group.

GUNS AND RIOTS

I think always being armed is a good thing, but pulling a gun out in the middle of a riot might not be the smartest idea. Unless you're physically being attacked, it's better to slip away unnoticed. Don't try to scare the crowd away with your gun.

Psychologically Destroy the Group

Fighting a large group doesn't mean you have to take on the entire crowd. Instead of physically defeating each attacker, your goal should be to to defeat them mentally by attempting to destroy their will to fight.

Your first strike must be spectacular and very visible to the group. The more visible the injury you inflict, the greater psychological effect it will have on the rest of the group. The first few seconds of the fight are critical; if you can psychologically defeat the group now, many of them will scatter without ever throwing a punch.

Make Every Hit Count

In a life-or-death situation, there are no rules. Take out their eyes, break their kneecaps, jab them in the throat with a makeshift weapon; do anything you can to win the battle. Your goal is to immobilize the attackers by any means available.

Identify the Leader

Who is the strongest link? In a riot situation this might be a little hard to tell, and in some cases there will probably be multiple instigators. But if you can determine the ringleader, this is the person you want to take out.

Taking out the leader can destroy the group's willingness to fight and is the first step to surviving an attack. Remember, you want to create a strong visible injury that will make the group rethink its attack.

(24) Surviving a Nuclear Disaster

When it comes to preparing for a nuclear disaster, there are three primary threats you need to consider. First is the threat of a nuclear weapons attack, most likely coming from a rogue nation with nothing to lose. Along that same line is the more likely limited nuclear threat posed by a dirty bomb. The third is the threat that's most often ignored or overlooked, and that is the threat in our own backyard, the threats posed by accidents at nuclear power plants.

HOW LIKELY IS A NUCLEAR DISASTER?

The threat of all-out nuclear war in America is probably pretty small because our nuclear arsenal ensures mutual destruction for the attacking country. That being said, it's not something we can ignore. The fact is, the world is a very dangerous place and there are a number of rogue nations that are doing everything they can to obtain nuclear weapons. In fact, China even released detailed plans, through their state media, on how they can strategically target the United States with nuclear bombs. So while the threat may be small, there are nations throughout the world that are actively planning to use this devastating type of warfare.

Dirty Bombs

A dirty bomb is a type of weapon that combines an explosive material with either a biochemical or radioactive material. In the case of radioactive dirty bombs, when the explosive is detonated, the blast pushes the radioactive material into the air, contaminating the immediate area. The degree of damage caused by a dirty bomb depends on a number of factors, including the type of radioactive material used, the size of the explosive, weather conditions, and where the bomb is detonated.

When people hear the term *radioactive bomb*, they often think of nuclear fallout and mass casualties. While some dirty bombs could potentially kill a fairly large amount of people, the main problem would likely be the public's reaction following the attack. The panic that would spread after this type of attack has the potential to not only change the way people live, but could be devastating to our economy. This makes detonating a dirty bomb every terrorist's dream, and terrorist organizations throughout the world are doing everything they can to make that dream become a reality.

The scary thing about this type of bomb is the fact that it doesn't take much expertise to build one. In fact, anyone who can build a conventional explosive weapon could theoretically build a dirty bomb, provided the radioactive material is attainable. The relative ease of constructing one of these explosive devices makes it incredibly likely that at some point a terrorist organization is going to set one off.

NUCLEAR POWER DISASTERS

While nuclear war and weapons might be scary, if you look at the history of nuclear technology, the biggest nuclear threat comes from accidents inside nuclear power plants. From Chernobyl and Three Mile Island, where mistakes led to the release of large amounts of radioactive material into the atmosphere, to the recent Fukushima Daiichi nuclear disaster that followed two large-scale natural disasters in Japan, the most immediate nuclear threat we face is the one in our own backyard.

There are currently over one hundred commercial nuclear reactors scattered throughout the United States. Many of these reactors have been allowed to operate far past their lifespan, and many have been plagued by problems that have been largely ignored by the mainstream media.

After watching events unfold in Japan, one thing became painfully clear: If you live anywhere near a nuclear power plant you need to be especially prepared for natural disasters, and you need to have an evacuation plan.

RECOGNIZING THE THREAT

Understanding the threat is the first step in being able to survive a potential nuclear disaster. That means being aware of what dangers are out there, and then using that knowledge to make a plan.

In the Case of Nuclear War

- **Keep an eye on the news.** It's very unlikely that a nuclear war will come by surprise. Keeping an eye on the news, and what countries are actively making threats, will give you a good idea of what threats actually exist and how to prepare for those threats.
- **Know the targets.** Major city centers and high-value military targets will be high on an enemy's list of targets. If a nuclear war is imminent, you want to have a plan that includes getting as far away as possible from any highly populated areas and major military bases.

In the Case of a Dirty Bomb

The goal of terrorists who would detonate a dirty bomb is to inflict as much damage as possible to increase public fear. Because they want mass casualties, they will most likely target crowded places, large urban centers, and highly publicized events.

- Avoid opening night events.
- Avoid sold-out shows and concerts.
- Avoid high-profile events and politically charged rallies.

In the Case of a Nuclear Power Plant Accident

- Identify the nuclear power plants close to your home. Even if they are hundreds of miles away, could fallout reach you through a contaminated river or typical weather patterns? These are the kinds of questions you need to start asking in order to determine your risk level.
- Identify any common natural disasters that could damage plants in your region. Earthquakes, tornadoes, flooding, and hurricanes all have the potential to wreak havoc on a nuclear power plant.

PREPARING FOR THE THREAT

Have an Evacuation Plan and a Bug Out Bag Ready to Go

The safest thing you can do is to get as far away from the nuclear threat as possible. Create an evacuation plan with multiple routes to a designated safe location. Keep bug out bags filled with necessary survival supplies stocked and ready to go at all times for every member of your household.

Stock Up on Essential Nuclear-Disaster Supplies

These supplies include

- duct tape
- thick plastic sheeting
- N95 particulate respirator masks
- plastic rain ponchos
- emergency medical supplies like potassium iodide pills

Prepare Your Shelter

If you have a basement, make sure it's stocked with food and water, a battery-powered radio (with extra batteries), flashlights, and any other emergency supplies that will be essential to your survival. Also, every inch of shielding that you can add to your shelter will further reduce your exposure to radiation. A heavy, solid material (like packed dirt, lead, thick walls, layers of rock, concrete, bricks, or any dense materials) between you and fallout is best. Stay indoors or below ground.

Start stocking up on food and water. Radioactive fallout can contaminate local food and water supplies for quite some time, so it's extremely important to have a stockpile of emergency food and water.

Stock up on sanitation items. It may not be pleasant to think about, but it's going to be even worse if you aren't prepared to deal with sanitation issues. Make sure you have garbage bags, cleaning supplies, and a portable camp toilet or a five-gallon bucket inside your shelter.

STEPS TO SURVIVE A NUCLEAR DISASTER
Evacuate

As I said, getting as far away from the disaster area is the safest thing you can do. Make evacuation your top priority and put your plan into place. If you are in the middle of an evacuation when the fallout starts to hit, immediately roll up your windows and turn off your air vents.

Surviving In the Fallout Zone

If evacuation wasn't an option or you find yourself inside the fallout zone, you need to take shelter.

- Immediately take shelter, preferably in a basement or underground concrete shelter. If that's not available, find anything that adds some sort of mass between you and the outside world.
- Turn off any kind of air conditioning or air-driven heating units and seal up the vents using plastic sheeting and duct tape from your stockpile.
- Seal all windows and doorways with plastic sheeting and duct tape, and stay indoors for at least forty-eight hours.
- Listen to local news reports, and try not to leave your shelter until the all clear has been given.

If There's a Possibility You Were Exposed to Radioactive Fallout

- Remove all clothing, including shoes, watches, and jewelry, before entering your shelter. Leave all these articles outside of the shelter. Bring nothing inside with you.
- If possible, hose yourself off before entering your shelter to remove any fallout that may be stuck to your skin or hair. If that's not an option shower as soon as you are inside the shelter.
- If you were exposed to fallout, you might want to start taking a round of potassium iodide pills.

(25) Surviving a Biochemical Attack

Biological and chemical weapons are among the top dangers we face and are some of the most dangerous weapons in the world. They are silent, deadly, and almost impossible to detect without high-tech equipment that, in most cases, is only available to government agencies.

HOW LIKELY IS A BIOCHEMICAL ATTACK?

Biochemical weapons are nothing new; in fact, the use of biochemical weapons dates back over one thousand years. One of the earliest recorded biochemical attacks occurred during the sixth century, when Assyrian forces poisoned enemy wells with ergot, a fungus that produces side effects similar to LSD.

Fast-forward to the twentieth century, where modern scientific methods and germ theory were used to develop and stockpile some of the most dangerous biological weapons the world has ever seen, and the race to see who could weaponize the most deadly germs and toxins was on.

These days, chemical weapons have become a huge concern because they can be quickly and easily made, even by those working in crude home laboratories. What was once a weapon that primarily concerned soldiers serving behind enemy lines has now become a very real threat that can affect anyone at any time.

As terrorist organizations throughout the world try to develop their own biochemical weapons, it's only a matter of time before one of these groups attempts to use it on the public.

HOW CAN YOU PREPARE FOR A BIOCHEMICAL ATTACK?

Preparing for a biochemical attack is going to be difficult. First, detecting biochemical agents with your five senses is almost impossible. Second, the equipment that can detect this type of threat is extremely expensive and is usually only available to law enforcement and government agencies.

While most detection equipment is probably out of your reach, there are some pieces of protective gear that you should think about keeping in your bug out bag:

- protective plastic clothing and gloves
- gas mask and/or N95 masks
- extra clothing sealed in plastic (to change into when you are safely away from the fallout)
- soap and water (to rinse off any chemicals that might be on your skin or in your eyes)
- a roll of duct tape, plastic sheeting and scissors (to seal off your shelter)

HOW CAN YOU MINIMIZE YOUR EXPOSURE TO AN ATTACK?

Be Aware of the Most Likely Targets

Public transportation, sporting events, malls, and anywhere that large groups of people congregate are all on the top of the target list for terrorists seeking to use a biochemical weapon.

Stay Vigilant While Attending Large Public Events

The people who use this type of weaponry are looking to inflict as much harm and gain as much media attention as they can. The only thing you can really do to stop the threat is to stay vigilant and watch out for anyone or anything that looks out of place.

Watch for Signs of Sudden Illness

In public places, if you notice a large number of people suddenly start to cough, gasp for air, rub their eyes, or become visibly sick, you need to act fast. Biochemical weapons are difficult to detect with your senses, but the side effects will quickly become apparent.

SURVIVING A BIOCHEMICAL ATTACK

Survival is going to depend on what chemical or biological agent was used and how quickly you can react to the situation.

If you have been exposed to a biochemical weapon attack, you need to remove yourself from the situation and remove as much of the agent as possible.

Get Away From the Fallout

If you can quickly determine where the weapon was deployed, immediately cover your face and head in the opposite direction, upwind from the fallout. If you can't determine where the weapon was set off, walk diagonally with the wind, trying to get as far away from the initial fallout zone as possible.

Find Shelter

Quickly find an area to shelter. Find anything you can to seal off doorways, windows, and vents to minimize the amount of exposure.

Remove Your Clothing

Clothing will likely be a major source of contamination. When taking off your shirt or coat, do not pull it over your head; instead rip, or cut the clothes off.

Wash Yourself Off

Washing your skin with soap and water will help eliminate a good portion of the chemical or biological agent. If your eyes are burning, rinse them out with pure water for ten to fifteen minutes.

Get Rid of Anything That has Been Exposed

Immediately bag and dispose of any clothing or items that were exposed to the chemical or biological agent.

Listen to News Reports

Once authorities find out exactly what chemical or biological agent was used, they will likely give further instructions that will be vital to your survival.

Surviving a Pandemic and Outbreak of Disease

One of the most likely large-scale threats, and one that has the very real possibility of being a global killer, is the threat of a pandemic outbreak. A pandemic outbreak is usually caused by a new virus, or a new strain of an existing virus, that the public has either no or very little immunity against.

HOW LIKELY IS A PANDEMIC?

Based on what we've seen throughout history, the threat of a pandemic is very real and very predictable—the way we live, travel, and buy our food makes us more susceptible to pandemics than any other time in the history of mankind. Places in this world that were once remote, and have active diseases that much of the world hasn't seen, are now only a plane trip away. It's not a matter of if it can happen; it's only a matter of when.

WHAT EFFECTS WOULD A PANDEMIC OUTBREAK HAVE ON THE WORLD?

Based on past pandemics, we know that millions upon millions of deaths is a real possibility. With the advent of modern technology and travel, that number will likely be much higher than anything we've ever seen.

During the 1918 flu pandemic over 500 million were infected, and it's estimated that 50 million of them died. Even in areas where mortality rates were relatively low, the population was still severely affected by the outbreak. Hospitals were quickly overwhelmed, schools were closed, and people had to make do with what they had in their homes because very few stores were open for business.

Be Prepared for the Entire System to Fail

From utilities and municipal water supplies to food delivery systems and every-day commerce, our technology-based infrastructure needs people to maintain the incredibly complex systems that we've grown so dependent on. As people start to become ill, those systems are going to quickly become overwhelmed. Without people to work, protect, and maintain our infrastructure I believe you will quickly see the entire system come to a screeching halt.

If we're not prepared to deal with it, the consequences of an infrastructure shutdown will likely kill more people than the actual pandemic.

WHAT CAN YOU DO TO MINIMIZE THE THREAT?

Pay Attention to News Reports

It's very unlikely that a pandemic will start in a developed part of the world. In all likelihood, it will begin in a region where sanitation and animal-handling standards are lower than we see in developed and modernized countries. If a pathogen starts to spread, those living in a modernized country will probably have at least a little bit of a warning. Any widespread outbreak of disease is going to make headlines.

Stockpile Emergency Supplies

During a pandemic outbreak, the best way to minimize your risk of becoming infected is to stay away from people. This means avoiding public places such as the grocery store, which is why you need to have enough food, water, and emergency supplies on hand to outlast the outbreak.

Previous pandemics have gone through communities in a matter of six to eight weeks, so keep that timeline in mind when planning for how much you need to buy.

Stay Clean and Practice Good Hygiene

As with all communicable diseases, the key to prevention lies in good hygiene. Hand washing is obvious, but even a simple alcohol-based hand sanitizer that contains over 70 percent alcohol can be enough to kill most pandemic pathogens. During a pandemic, carry hand sanitizer with you and apply it any time you touch a commonly handled item such as a door, light switch, public countertop, and money.

Don't re-wear any clothing you have worn outside of the house during the outbreak without washing it in a bleach solution first. Regularly use alcohol or bleach-based cleaners to wipe down frequently touched surfaces in your home during an outbreak (doorknobs, light switches, sink faucets, etc.)

Keep Social Distance When in Public

The best way to improve your chances of staying healthy during an outbreak is to practice social distancing. This means limiting your contact with others and staying at least six feet away from people if you do have to go out.

STEPS TO SURVIVE THE OUTBREAK

If a pandemic reaches your area, here are some things you can do to increase your odds of surviving.

Avoid Hospitals and Shelters

If you're sick, then by all means you probably need to consult with a medical professional for advice. That being said, hospitals will be ground zero in the war and should be avoided if possible. Avoid shelters or any area where large groups of people are gathered.

Stay at Home and Away From the Public

Limiting your exposure to other people will limit your exposure to any type of disease. Don't go out unless absolutely necessary.

Wear a Mask

If you absolutely have to go out, wear a mask. Masks are a last resort. They cannot be relied on to stop infection. Respirators are designed to help reduce, not eliminate, exposure to the infection. With that being said, I would not leave the house during an outbreak without wearing an N95 particulate respirator mask.

Surviving a Power Grid Failure

(27)

Over the last decade, large portions of the United States' power grid have gone down. From the great Northeast blackout of 2003, which plunged more than fifty million people into darkness, to the 2011 Southwest blackout that left nearly seven million people without power, our power grid has experienced some major problems that are very likely to happen again.

HOW REAL ARE THE THREATS TO THE POWER GRID?
Natural Disasters
Every year storms routinely wreak havoc on our grid, severely damaging power lines and putting major stress on a system that's already strained under normal conditions. When Hurricane Sandy slammed the East Coast of the United States in 2012, we witnessed how bad the problems have become. Over 1.3 million people were plunged into darkness, forced to go without power for over a week. In some of the affected areas it actually took over a month to restore the power.

Since natural disasters like hurricanes, earthquakes, tornadoes, and winter storms happen on a routine basis, the reality of the situation is that until the power companies start better protecting our nation's aging power grid, we will likely see larger and lengthier power outages for some time to come.

Cyber Attacks
In the future, and to some extent even now, wars are going to be largely fought in cyberspace. With little more than a keyboard and a bit of malicious code, a nation's infrastructure can easily be targeted and taken down—all without ever having to fire a single shot or drop a single bomb.

But it's not just government infrastructure that we have to worry about. Hackers are becoming so sophisticated that they now routinely penetrate some of our nation's most secure systems. Banks, Internet companies, and even critical communications infrastructure have all been successfully targeted and penetrated by hackers. In my opinion, it's only a matter of time before one of them is able to do some serious damage to our power grid.

Terrorist Attacks

While very rarely reported, numerous portions of key infrastructure have either been infiltrated or probed by terrorists. Because cyber threats have become such a concern, many government agencies have ignored how much damage can be done by seemingly low-tech attacks. In fact, in 2013 an unknown group of attackers was able to penetrate a San Jose, California, power substation. The group was able to cut fiber lines and then fire off over a hundred shots with a high-power rifle into ten transformers.

With so many power stations spread throughout the country, many of them completely unguarded, these low-tech style attacks can be incredibly successful, making them a prime tactic for terrorists.

Solar Flares and Coronal Mass Ejections

Back in 1859, when the world was just starting to experiment with electricity, a massive solar flare (followed by a coronal mass ejection, or CME) slammed into the Earth, frying telegraph systems and severely shocking telegraph operators across the country. There weren't many electronic devices back then to worry about, but if a flare of that size hit today, entire electrical grids could be fried in the blink of an eye.

In fact, back in March 1989, a much smaller flare wiped out five major electricity transmission lines in Quebec, leaving a huge number of Canadians without power for almost twenty-four hours. Had the flare been slightly larger, it could have caused widespread transformer damage that would have cut power for weeks, maybe longer.

Despite huge advances in technology, today's power grid and many of the fancy gadgets our society has become dependent on are incredibly vulnerable to large solar flares and CMEs that could wipe out an entire grid almost instantly. In a matter of minutes, life as we know it would start to look a lot like the nineteenth century.

Electromagnetic Pulse

Although this is probably one of the least likely threats, there are a number of nations that possess the ability to detonate an electromagnetic pulse (EMP) blast that could shut down an entire country's power grid.

The effects of an EMP are pretty similar to what would be experienced after a large-scale solar flare or CME, except far more electronic devices would likely be damaged because an EMP has the ability to destroy devices that aren't even connected to power lines.

LIMITING YOUR RISK OF POWER OUTAGES
Natural Disaster Power Outages

You can't stop nature, but you can take steps to limit the amount of damage it can do. Most weather-related power outages are caused by falling trees. Dead limbs and dead trees are most susceptible to high-wind damage. Removing vulnerable trees from your property and requesting your neighbors do the same, especially if their trees are at risk of falling on your property and causing damage is a good first step. Trim back any branches that are near power lines directly leading to your home, even if the branches are alive.

NEVER RUN AN EMERGENCY GENERATOR INDOORS

An emergency generator can make life a lot easier during an outage, but a generator's exhaust fumes contain carbon monoxide, which can kill you in a matter of minutes. When running a generator, make sure it's outside and away from windows and vents.

Cyber Attack Related Outages

Stay up to date. Hackers often depend on other people to successfully pull off their attacks. By penetrating home computers, a hacker can create entire networks that simultaneously attack their intended target. To make sure you're not part of the problem, keep your computer's software up-to-date and make sure you install antivirus software and a firewall on all of your computers.

PREPARING FOR A POWER GRID FAILURE
Stock Up on Emergency Food and Water

If you are able to stay in your home after the grid goes down, there's probably a good chance your municipal water is going to become undrinkable. There's an even better chance that your local grocery stores will be stripped bare in a matter of hours. Do you really want to be one of the unprepared masses fighting for the last bottle of water?

Stock Up on Camping Supplies

When people ask me what kind of survival supplies they should stock up on, I tell them to pretend they're going camping. The same type of gear you would bring on a camping trip (the kind of camping trip that doesn't include staying in a fully powered RV park) is the same type of equipment that will come in handy during a power outage.

- Lighting: Flashlights, lanterns, and candles are all emergency essentials you can never have enough of.
- Batteries: Stock up on as many as you can, preferably rechargeable ones that can be charged with a small solar charger. Don't forget the solar charger!
- Battery-powered radio (even better, a shortwave or ham radio)
- Sleeping bags (depending on the weather)
- First aid kits
- Extra medication
- Outdoor barbeque, fire pit, or camping stove for cooking

28

Surviving a Cyber Attack and Hackers

Over the last fifty years, the world has witnessed some of the greatest advances in energy, information technology, and modern infrastructure the world has ever seen. Unfortunately, these same advances have opened up somewhat of a Pandora's box, exposing the world to threats and vulnerabilities that no one could have imagined a few short decades ago.

Despite what governments may actually admit to, almost every developed country in the world is under attack. But this new type of warfare is not being fought on the battlefields, it's being fought in cyberspace by an enemy that is incredibly difficult to detect and defeat.

The attacks in cyberspace are being launched by military cyber teams, terrorist organizations, and anonymous hacker groups. Even scarier is the fact that a lone hacker, with the right know-how and resources, can singlehandedly take down entire power grids, financial systems, and other vital infrastructure.

The attacks are targeting both government systems and private corporations but can also affect private individuals who are at risk of identity theft, cleaned out bank accounts, and threats that haven't even been thought of yet. This new frontier in warfare is extremely dangerous, and in my opinion, we have only begun to see what's really possible.

CYBER ATTACKS ON INFASTRUCTURE

Throughout the world, vital infrastructure like energy, telecommunications, and transportation systems are incredibly vulnerable to attack and are being targeted twenty-four hours a day, seven days a week.

To get an idea of how serious the threat is, you need to understand what is being targeted and what would happen if one of these systems was maliciously penetrated.

There are a number of critical infrastructure sectors that are ripe for attack:

- agriculture and food
- banking and finance
- chemical
- critical manufacturing
- dams
- defense
- emergency services
- energy
- government facilities
- information technology
- nuclear reactors and waste
- public health and healthcare
- telecommunications
- transportation systems
- water and water treatment systems

Many of these sectors are controlled by SCADA (Supervisory Control and Data Acquisition) systems, which were previously thought impenetrable. Unfortunately, recent events suggest that might not be the case.

In a 2013 report prepared for the Department of Homeland Security, engineers proved they could penetrate and shut down almost every major industrial control system they tested. These findings were a real wake-up call, but were only the tip of the iceberg.

Even systems that were once thought impenetrable because they supposedly lacked connections to the outside world have been attacked using highly sophisticated computer worms that took advantage of vulnerabilities in Windows-based systems used to program industrial control systems.

It's really only a matter of time before some hacker, terrorist organization, or rogue world government uses these vulnerabilities to target multiple critical infrastructure sectors. When this happens, all hell is going to break loose.

A coordinated attack on any of these critical infrastructure sectors could bring a country or the entire world to its knees. Imagine a scenario where someone was able to shut down either part or all of a nation's power grid, while at the same time disabling telecommunication systems and other key infrastructure. Now are you starting to get a picture of how bad things can get?

HOW CAN YOU PROTECT YOURSELF FROM A CYBER ATTACK?

While there's probably very little you can do to prevent a large-scale cyber attack on the infrastructure, the average person can do a lot to protect him or herself on a personal level.

Update Electronic Operating Systems

Make sure the operating systems of your personal computers, tablets, and smartphones are always up-to-date. This is one of the best things you can do to protect yourself, and to some extent, the rest of the world. When patches or operating system upgrades are released, install them as soon as possible. Installing the updates can limit your vulnerability to attack by people who have discovered holes in older operating systems.

Install an Antivirus Program and Keep It Up-to-Date

Even surfing what may seem like a completely safe website can be like playing a game of electronic Russian roulette. Some of the largest and most well-known websites in the world have been hacked, increasing the possibility of your computer being affected with malicious code.

Limit the Information You Share Online

We are living in an age in which everyone seems to want to share his or her life story online. But if you wouldn't tell a stranger on the street this information, why would you consider sharing it online where the entire world can see? Keep in mind that every piece of data, thought, or information you share online is out there forever. You can never get it back, and you can never undo what's been done.

Don't Trust Anyone on the Internet

Beware of anything that looks or feels suspicious. Even something as innocent as a USB device that someone gives you can be a clever attempt to spread malicious code and infect an entire network. This is especially true if you work in a high-risk industry with tight Internet security. Criminal hackers will target unknowing employees in the hopes of penetrating these closed networks.

HOW TO SURVIVE A CYBER ATTACK

Preparing for a widespread cyber attack is really no different than preparing for any other type of disaster where you may be without essential services for an extended period of time. The plans you created using the information in chapter two will help you prepare for the chaos you'll likely face as a result of a large-scale cyber attack.

29

Surviving a Water Infrastructure Problem

In addition to providing clean, drinkable water to the public, the public water systems also deal with things like storm water runoff and waste water treatment, and provide water to the agriculture industry. Our public water systems are probably one of our most important resources, yet most people completely ignore how valuable and vulnerable this natural resource is.

In the United States alone, there are over 160,000 public water systems, which provide drinking water to more than 300 million Americans. Disruptions in these systems would not only cause a severe public health and safety hazard but could also cause considerable economic losses.

THREATS TO WATER INFRASTRUCTURE

Threats to the water supply have plagued those who maintain public water systems since their beginning. Some of these threats include

- industrial pollution and contamination of waterways
- the threat of bioterrorism or chemical sabotage
- natural disaster-related problems like floods or storm pipe discharges
- agricultural runoff and pesticides
- power outages that can affect water treatment plants
- aging infrastructure that can fail
- hackers (the newest threat) who threaten the entire system

Industrial Pollution and Contamination

Business and industry pose one of the top threats to the world's water infrastructure. A recent example happened in early 2014, when an industrial accident contaminated the Elk River in West Virginia with a hazardous chemical, contaminating almost a quarter of the state's water supply. As a result, almost 300,000 people were told not to drink, cook, or wash with the local tap water.

Almost immediately, every store within a 100-mile (161 km) radius of the affected area completely sold out of water. For over a week, residents were unable to use the water coming out of their faucets—they couldn't even use it to wash their hands. People were in full-blown panic mode, all because they thought it could never happen. They became complacent, believing the water would always be there when they needed it.

Terrorist Threats to Our Water Supply

One look at what happened in West Virginia shows you just how vulnerable our water supply is. If a small chemical leak released into a river could cause so much trouble, imagine what would happen if a terrorist released an even more deadly chemical agent or biological toxin that went undetected.

It's no secret that terrorists have been trying to target our public water systems for quite some time. In fact, over the last ten years, public water systems throughout the United States have been targeted, and in some cases even penetrated, by people looking to threaten this key infrastructure.

In 2004, the FBI and the Department of Homeland Security issued a bulletin warning that terrorists were trying to recruit workers at water utilities as part of a plan to poison our drinking water. This and a number of similar threats throughout the world only act to remind us how many people are looking to do us harm.

An attack on our water system has the potential to kill millions of people; some will die because of the dangerous toxins, others because they were unprepared to survive an extended water emergency.

Natural Disaster-Related Threats

Another concern, one that we see play out even during small-scale storms, is how quickly our public water systems can become overwhelmed by natural disasters.

Main breaks, power failures, and equipment failures during a natural disaster can quickly cause a local water supply to become undrinkable. Natural disasters can also cause chemical leaks, storm sewer discharges, and pathogens to overwhelm a city's water treatment plants.

PREPARING FOR WATER-RELATED PROBLEMS

Next to the air that we breathe, water is the most important element to man's survival. So having a clean supply of water is essential to our health, safety, and well-being. A person can survive without food for over a month, but without water our bodies can only survive for a couple of days.

To be prepared for a water emergency, store at least one gallon (4 L) of water per person per day. In general, a moderately active person needs at least two quarts (half a gallon, or 2 L) of water daily just for drinking. Keep in mind this can vary depending on age, physical condition, activity level, diet, and climate. You'll need additional water for sanitation each day.

To determine your exact water needs, take the following into account:

- Store a minimum of one gallon (4 L) of water per person per day, for drinking and sanitation.
- Children, nursing mothers, and those with medical conditions may need more water.
- If you live in a warm climate, be aware that your water needs can double.
- Store at least a fourteen-day supply of water per person in your household.
- Invest in a high-quality water filtration system and keep a gallon (4 L) of unscented liquid household chlorine bleach for sanitation and water purification purposes.

LONG-TERM WATER STORAGE

The storage containers you choose will largely depend on the amount of space you have to work with. With any type of water storage, you'll want to put your containers in a cool dark area that does not receive direct sunlight.

Water Bottles

When looking for water bottles, find ones that are made out of high-quality food-grade materials. I would advise against using ordinary milk jugs, as they don't last as long as other bottles and are almost impossible to completely clean.

I have found that ordinary two-liter soda bottles are a good, inexpensive option for water storage. They are small, easy to tuck away, and can be easily carried in a backpack when staying in one place is not an option.

Water Barrels

Fifty-five-gallon (208 L) water barrels are a pretty common option for survival-ists, and they should be pretty easy to find at most sporting goods stores. These barrels are usually blue (this is more of a safety thing that lets you know water is stored inside) and are made with heavy-duty food-grade plastic materials.

Tanks and Cisterns

Another popular option for storing water is a freestanding tank or cistern. These tanks are popular in rural areas that don't have access to public water utilities.

These offer the added benefit of being able to catch rainwater by hooking them up to your rooftop gutter systems. If you can afford to install a roof catch-ment system, this is an excellent option for long-term survival retreats, and it can really go a long way to solving a lot of your water problems.

MAKING CONTAMINATED WATER SAFE TO DRINK

Even the best emergency plan needs a Plan B. When it comes to water storage, this means knowing how to find and sanitize water.

While there are a number of options for cleaning contaminated water, none of them is 100 percent effective at treating everything. The best methods for killing bacteria and other microorganisms include boiling, filtering, and chemi-cal treatments.

Boiling

Boiling is the safest and easiest method of treating water that's contaminated with microorganisms. That being said, keep in mind it will not remove chemicals, heavy metals, or salts.

While some "survival experts" advise boiling your water for ten minutes, the truth is, most bacteria and microorganisms are killed once the water reaches its boiling point (212° F, 100° C). I advise waiting for it come to a rolling boil, and then letting it boil for at least one minute to be safe.

Filtering

In my opinion, a water filter is one of the most important pieces of gear you can have. There are a number of quality water filters on the market, but there are a couple that you might want to consider first.

Berkey water filter. The Berkey water purification system is a popular at-home filter in the survivalist community. The Berkey can remove viruses, pathogenic bacteria, cysts, and can even filter out chemicals.

Hiking filters. One of the best portable water filters that I've found is the Katadyn Pocket Water Microfilter. While this is one of the more expensive hiking filters on the market, it's also the most reliable. This little filter can handle over 13,000 gallons (49,210 L) of water and will filter all microorganisms larger than 0.2 microns. Its small size also makes it easily fit into any bug out bag or survival kit.

SteriPENs. A SteriPEN uses ultraviolet light to eliminate over 99.9 percent of bacteria, viruses, and protozoa that cause waterborne illness. They are small, lightweight, and can easily be carried in your pocket or bug out bag.

Chemical Treatments

There are two main types of chemical water treatments: those using iodine and those using chlorine.

Iodine treatment. Most iodine tablets or products will give you instructions on how to use their product, so make sure you follow the manufacture's instructions when using the product to treat water.

When using a liquid 2 percent tincture of iodine, add five drops per quart (1 L) when the water is clear. Add ten drops per quart (1 L) when the water is cloudy. Wait thirty minutes if the water is warm and an hour if it's hot outside. Some people are allergic to iodine so be aware that it may not be suitable for all people.

Chlorine treatment. Chlorine tablets can be another effective way to treat most pathogens. Just like iodine tablets, make sure you follow all manufacturers' instructions when using the product to treat water.

Water can also be treated with ordinary household bleach. Add ⅛ of a teaspoon (or 8 drops) of unscented liquid household chlorine bleach per gallon (4 L) of water. Never use scented bleaches, color-safe bleaches, or bleaches with added cleaners or chemicals.

Surviving a Major Food Crisis

Access to adequate food supplies is a growing concern and something that is critical to survival in an emergency situation. Food emergencies can quickly become a problem during most regional disasters because of complex food delivery systems that have left us vulnerable to food shortages caused by delivery disruptions that often happen during a crisis situation.

Modern-day grocery stores have very limited storage capacity. Rather than having large stocks of food on hand, stores rely on a "just in time" system of food distribution, which means the food on the shelves is the only food in the store. When the shelves are emptied, they will stay empty until the next delivery arrives. This leaves most major cities only a few days away from starvation if distribution is stopped. In fact, during even small-scale disasters entire cities can quickly become food deserts, as unprepared people strip grocery store shelves bare in order to feed their families during the crisis.

WHAT WOULD CAUSE A FOOD CRISIS?

Some scenarios that can cause a food emergency include

- a natural disaster that can stop or slow down deliveries into the affected areas
- environmental conditions such as drought, flooding, or insect infestations that can wipe out crops and put livestock at risk
- disruption or collapse of the food distribution network through either union strikes or economic collapse
- a major or sudden fuel shortage, which shuts down delivery trucks
- food safety concerns and disease outbreaks such as E. coli and salmonella

- armed conflicts, wars, or political disturbances
- terrorist attacks with biological agents

People Compound the Problem

It's easy to put the problem on modern business practices, but the fact is, average citizens are just as guilty in compounding the food security problem. Most people only have a couple of day's worth of food stored in their own homes, which is why you see so much chaos in the lead up to and aftermath of any disaster. People have become complacent, believing the store shelves will always be full and there will always be enough food to feed their families.

PROTECTING YOURSELF FROM A FOOD SHORTAGE

The good news is there is a lot you can do to protect yourself from a food shortage.

Increase Your Food Supplies

You simply can't rely on the current food distribution system to be there when you need it. The best thing you can do to protect yourself from disruptions is to start stockpiling your own inventory of food.

- Calculate exactly how much food your family consumes in a day, and come up with a menu plan that allows you to have at least a two-week supply of emergency food on hand at all times.
- Set aside a dedicated area in your home where you can build up a stockpile of emergency food. If you live in an area prone to earthquakes or flooding, you may want to split your supply up and store it in separate areas of your home. That way you limit your supply's exposure to disaster-related damage.
- Few people's budgets allow them to buy an extra two weeks worth of food all at once. This can sometimes become a stumbling block that makes people give up on preparedness; don't let it discourage you from being prepared. You can build your supply over time. Start by picking up a couple extra canned goods, dried foods, and other essential

supplies every time you go to the store. See chapter three for more details on how to store food.

In my opinion, two weeks is the absolute minimum amount of supplies that you should have on hand at all times, and even that's a very conservative number. Once you hit your goal of having two weeks' worth of food on hand, you should then set a goal for having a three-month supply, then six-month, and then twelve-month supply of food.

Buy Locally

Supporting local farmers and food co-ops can do a lot to maintain local food supplies. Almost every community has some sort of local food co-op or farmers market that can be a great resource for cutting your reliance on the system.

Learn How to Grow Your Own Food

Being prepared for a food crisis is so much more than just stockpiling food. To be truly prepared, you must learn how to be self-sufficient. Even a small backyard garden can help add to your food supplies and can do a lot to ensure your ability to feed your family should local food supplies run low.

Learn How to Can and Preserve to Make Your Harvest Last Longer

Food preservation techniques like canning and dehydrating foods can help you build your survival stockpiles at a fraction of the cost. By learning these age-old food preservation methods, you cut your reliance on the system and begin to ensure your family's food security.

Learn How to Hunt and Fish

Being able to provide for your family is not something that should be taken lightly. Even in urban areas, you're probably within a couple of hours of somewhere where you can hunt and fish. Learning how to obtain your own food from nature is one of the best things you can do to guarantee your food security.

PART FIVE:
Surviving Financial and Economic Threats

For those who regularly visit my website, Off Grid Survival, it's probably not going to be a huge surprise that I devoted an entire chapter to financial preparedness. I believe that the economy is one of the most immediate and dangerous problems facing the United States and many other countries worldwide. In my opinion, economic problems should be on the top of everyone's list of most likely disasters.

Of all the situations discussed in this book, financial disaster is probably one of the most likely emergencies you'll face. From extreme examples like the collapse of a country's economy to everyday financial problems like job losses or unexpected medical issues that can quickly push a family into economic ruin, the fact is, financial problems are something that will, at some point, affect every single one of us.

While preparing for economic problems might not be sexy—how many Hollywood disaster movies focus on someone who just lost his job and now has to worry about feeding his family?—the fact is, the world is heading toward some major economic problems. If you want to survive what's coming, now is the time to start taking these problems seriously.

The three financial preparedness principles outlined in this section—setting a budget, prepping on a budget, and developing a plan for long-term financial security—are critical to self-reliance. They also provide a foundation for surviving the financial emergencies covered in this section—surviving a job loss, a recession, and total economic collapse.

Setting a Budget

One of the most common excuses I hear from people who have failed to take preparedness seriously is often one of financial burden. When asking people why they don't prepare, I often hear the excuse, "I don't have money to waste on preparedness; I'm barely scraping by as it is."

Ironically, these same people usually have more than enough money for their $5 lattes before work, fast-food lunches, and takeout dinners on the way home.

You can immediately see what's going on, but therein lies the problem; most people don't take the time to really look at what they're actually spending. As simple as it sounds, to get ahold of your financial future, the first thing you have to do is sit down and set a written budget. For a lot of people making a budget ranks right up there with death, taxes, and public speaking. They seem to think that by establishing a budget, they're somehow going to have to suffer through life without ever having any kind of fun. Others avoid it because they know what they're going to find, and the thought of having to take responsibility scares the hell out of them.

The only way you're going to get ahead and secure your future, is to start telling your money what to do. Establishing a written budget ensures that every dollar you make works for you, not against you.

The act of establishing a budget doesn't have to be some complex accounting spreadsheet that only your CPA can understand. In fact, your budget should really only have of two basic parts:

1. what's coming in (all sources of income)
2. what's going out (all expenses)

It's really that simple.

How to Create a Written Budget

- On one page, list every source of income. This will include obvious things like income from your job, and not so obvious things like side jobs, residual income, or things you sell online and gifts of money.
- On a separate page, write down every single expense you have for the coming month: rent, insurance, car payments, meals, and entertainment. Every dollar needs to be accounted for. Keep receipts for cash transactions and use statements for debit and credit cards to account for everything. Even your monthly savings, your investments, and your extra debt payments should have a line item in your budget.
- When you have both your incoming and outgoing pages complete, your income minus your outgoing expenses should equal zero. If you have anything left over in either category, you are not budgeting correctly.

The first thing most people find when they start budgeting is the numbers sometimes don't add up. On paper it may seem like you actually have a surplus of money. If that happens, you probably weren't being honest with what you're actually spending, and you may have to dig out last month's receipts or review your past bank statements. But don't worry; this is where you can start to change your life and secure your financial future.

How to Use a Budget to Cut Your Expenses

Once you sit down and actually start accounting for where your dollars are going, you should be able to start cutting back on your monthly expenses. I'm not saying you have to completely stop spending, but you need to have a dollar amount set in your budget for every type of expense. These questions can help you find places to make cuts in your expenses.

- **Are there areas in your budget you can cut out?** You're probably spending a huge amount of money on nonessential things that you could do without or get for less by making them at home. Look at dining out, entertainment, and snacks and drinks you pick up while you're out.
- **Can you downgrade?** Many at-home services such as cable TV, Internet service, and cell phone plans come in a variety of pricing options. Down-

grading to a lower priced plan, switching to another provider, or eliminating the service all together can significantly lower your monthly expenses.

- **Are there coupons?** You don't have to spend hours clipping coupons or become one of those extreme couponers, but you should take advantage of every chance you can get to save money. Most major food manufacturers offer money-saving coupons through their websites, Facebook pages, or other online resources.
- **Consider bartering.** Do you have a special skill or talent that might be useful to others? There are a number of bartering websites online where you can offer your services in exchange for things you might need. Websites like craigslist, freecycle.org, and Facebook groups are all a great resource for bartering.

EASY WAYS TO STICK TO YOUR BUDGET

Use Cash Only

Cash-only payments have two benefits:

- You experience the actual loss of giving over physical money.
- It prevents you from spending money you don't have.

Study after study has shown that people spend far more money when they're able to purchase something electronically—with a credit or debit card. Retailers and bankers know this; that's why today, even debit cards are starting to offer perks and reward points. They're all banking on the hope that you won't realize what you're really spending.

Try the Envelope Budgeting System

This is a great way to visualize the money you have available in each of your budget categories and can be particularly helpful for those having trouble sticking to a written budget.

Assign an envelope to each category in your monthly budget—food, utilities, rent, preparedness, etc. At the beginning of every month, place the amount of cash designated to the category in its envelope. Use the envelope to pay for these items throughout the month. When an envelope runs out of cash, you're done spending in that category for the month. The simple act of dividing your money into these envelopes has a powerful psychological effect and can help you stop overspending on certain parts of your budget—especially on things like fast food and entertainment.

Prepping on a Budget

One common, and big, misconception about preparedness is that it takes loads of cash to be fully and properly prepared for survival. In my experience, nothing could be further from the truth. In fact, having a lot of money to spend on survival can sometimes become a crutch that actually impedes a person's ability to become truly self-reliant. Don't get me wrong, I love my gear as much as the next guy, and good gear sure does make life a lot easier during a crisis. But survival gear also has a big downside, which is the fact that it can be dangerous, even deadly, to become too reliant on your gear.

Many people make the mistake of believing they can buy their way out of danger. They spend countless amounts of money stocking up on commercial survival foods, buying prepackaged first aid kits, and ordering all sorts of survival gear that looks like it's right out of some bad Hollywood sci-fi flick. They make the mistake of believing large amounts of gear will somehow save them when things go bad.

The truth is prepping can be done very successfully with little to no budget. Those who prepare with knowledge will be far better off than those who rely solely on their gear to survive. Knowledge is the key to surviving in just about any situation. That being said, there are some advantages and practicalities to stockpiling food, water, and some basic survival supplies.

Adding a "Preparedness" line item in your budget is no different from making a monthly insurance policy payment on your home, car, or health. Preparedness is the best insurance policy you can buy. It not only ensures you'll be able to take care of your family during an emergency, but it also protects you from things like economic problems, a job loss, or an extended illness that might cause a loss of income. Before arbitrarily picking an amount to spend on prepping each month, take the time to analyze your budget to determine how much money you can safely spend on building your preparedness supplies.

TIPS FOR PREPPING ON A BUDGET
Take an Inventory of Your Current Supplies
Most of us have more gear and equipment than we realize, and chances are you already have a number of things in your home that can be used during an emergency situation. Having a good inventory of your current supplies will prevent you from buying something you may already have.

Gradually Purchase Your Supplies Over Time
A lot of people mistakenly think they need to do everything at once. If they can't have it now, they often become discouraged or give up all together. While most people don't have the financial means to buy everything at once, that doesn't mean you should give up on preparedness. Build your supplies when you can. If it means buying one extra can of food every time you go to the grocery store, then start with one can. Even that one extra can of food, purchased on a regular basis, will quickly add up. If you want to make a larger gear purchase, you may need to set aside a portion of your monthly preparedness money for a few months until you have enough to make the large purchase.

Don't Buy Commercial Survival Foods
Over the last couple of years, emergency food companies have sprung up everywhere. Personally, I really don't enjoy the taste of most of these products. I think I'd rather eat dog food over some of the commercial survival foods I've tried. Another problem is they can be very costly. Stockpiling even a couple of months' worth of commercial survival food can cost thousands of dollars for a single person. Now add up all the members in your family and most people would be hard-pressed to find that kind of money just lying around the house.

Many first-time preppers make the mistake of stockpiling foods that they would never eat in a non-survival situation simply because the food is marketed as being specifically for emergency survival. During times of crisis, do you really want to start eating foods that may disagree with your body? In my opinion, you will be far better off stocking up on shelf-stable foods that you already eat.

Take Advantage of Sales and Coupons

Again, you don't have to spend hours upon hours clipping coupons, but you should take advantage of every chance you can get to save money. Most major food manufacturers offer money-saving coupons through their websites, Facebook pages, or other online resources and local newspapers. A few minutes of work every week can save you thousands of dollars throughout the course of a year.

Stock Up on Knowledge

Most survival situations can be prevented or survived by learning basic survival skills. If you're short on funds, compensate by stocking up on knowledge. It's the one thing that can't be taken away and it will always be there when you need it. I suggest taking the time to read as many survival books and websites as you can get your hands on. To stay on top of the latest survival techniques, skills, gear, and threat assessments I also suggest following me at my website, offgridsurvival.com

Spend Time, Not Money

While knowledge is a key aspect of survival, taking the time to practice your skills is a key part of the survival puzzle. Training so you can master survival skills is what makes the difference between success and failure (life or death). To really be able to count on your knowledge during a crisis, run through your techniques in a number of scenarios and environments. The more you train in real-world situations, the more likely you'll be able to perform your skills when it really matters.

- Take the time to role-play certain survival situations, such as what you would do during each of the specific disaters you identified in your threat assessment.

- Hiking, backpacking, and backcountry camping can all help prepare you for the mental challenges associated with survival. They also can help prepare your body for the rigorous challenges associated with some survival situations, especially those that might require an evacuation by foot.
- Turn ordinary events into a time to practice your skills. For instance, when doing something like grilling out in your backyard, use this time as a way to practice how you would cook during a grid-down situation where you may lose the ability to cook inside your home. Practice building a fire pit and starting your fire with different fire-starting techniques.

Develop a Plan for Long-Term Financial Security

If you take one thing away from this book, I hope it's a greater sense of self-reliance. In any kind of emergency, the only people you can truly count on are yourself and your immediate family. Yes, there are millions of good and caring people in this world, but that doesn't mean they're going to be there for you when you need them. One important part of becoming self-reliant is developing a plan for long-term financial security. Here are some steps you can take.

STOP BEING A SLAVE TO DEBT

Going into debt makes you a slave to your debt holder and puts you into a position where your money becomes your master. From this day forward, plan on never buying anything on credit again. Adjust your budget to pay down your debt as fast as possible. Try tackling one debt at a time while maintaining minimum payments on your other debts until all your debts are eliminated.

ESTABLISH AN EMERGENCY FUND

Life rarely goes as planned. From those unexpected vehicle repairs that seem to hit at the worst possible moment to the recent unemployment surge, there seems to be a never-ending supply of financial turmoil. When things go bad financially, it can sometimes feel like the end of the world for those who are in the middle of the crisis. When it comes to preparing for economic troubles, one of the best possible steps you can take is to establish an emergency fund. Your emergency fund should be split into three main categories:

1. Cash-on-hand fund: You need a ready supply of cash at all times. In the wake of an emergency, banks won't be open and cards won't be accepted if the grid is down. You'll need cash to pay for things like supplies, fuel, hotel rooms during an evacuation, etc. Natural disasters, power grid failures, and sudden evacuations can happen anywhere with little notice. Keep cash on hand and invest in a secure wall safe to keep this fund safe in your home.

2. Short-term fund: Your short-term fund is the fund you go to when you have an immediate emergency. It can be used to pay for smaller emergencies, like an unexpected vehicle repair or replacing a major appliance that stopped working. This should be kept at a local bank and have a debit card attached to the account so you can immediately access your money.

Short-term funds can also be used to get you through larger events where it may take a couple of days to access your long-term emergency fund.

3. Long-term fund: This is a reserve of money that can get you through long-term difficulties like a job loss, or get you back on your feet after something like a major natural disaster. While this fund should be kept where you can access it quickly, it shouldn't be so easily accessible that you'll be tempted to use it for everyday spending. This fund should be able to see you through at least six months of regular expenses and should be placed in a savings or money market account. Remember this is an insurance policy, not an investment fund, so you should not be worried about making money on this account.

BUILD A STOCKPILE OF LONG-TERM GOODS

One of the best and easiest ways to prepare for the future is to start stockpiling consumable resources. I'm not talking about running out and buying a bunch of useless crap, but instead stocking up on things you'll need and will hold their value in the future.

When building a stockpile of goods, look for things you can't produce yourself, things that will hold their value indefinitely, and things you can use to survive during times of trouble. Some ideas of what to stockpile:

Food and Water

This is really a no-brainer. Without these two items, the rest of the list really becomes unnecessary. The first thing on anyone's list should be making sure they have enough food and water to sustain themselves and their family through any kind of disaster. If you experience a job loss, you can eat the food in your stockpile and save the money you would normally spend on groceries. You can also eat one or two meals a week from your stockpile to stretch your grocery budget in tight months and to keep the food from spoiling.

Guns and Ammo

The last few years have shown that guns and ammunition can be hard to come by during uncertain times. For instance, after the presidential election in 2012 it became almost impossible to find .22lr ammunition anywhere in the United States, and two years later it's still incredibly hard to find. So, not only are guns and ammunition important for survival reasons, but they also are great investments that will hold their value even during a crisis.

Tools

During the Great Depression, those who could fix things themselves were usually the ones who survived. Having a good stockpile of tools, combined with the knowledge of how to use them, is not only a good investment but can also ensure you have a method for generating income. If things ever completely collapse in this country, those who are able to fix things are going to be some of the most sought after people in the new economy. You'll also be able to repair your own belongings when they break so you don't have to purchase new ones.

DIY Items

Along with tools, start thinking about items that will help you become more self-sufficient. This can be anything from sewing machines for making new clothing to gardening and hunting supplies that will help you feed your family.

Basic Necessities

Clothing, first aid supplies, and anything that is a legitimate necessity are all things that you should start thinking about stockpiling.

Stockpile Knowledge

Knowledge really is the key to survival. The best thing you can do to secure your survival and your financial future is to start accumulating skills that will be important during a collapse. These skills include

- **DIY skills.** During a full-blown economic collapse, one of the most important skills you can have is the ability to do it yourself. Start taking the time to learn how to fix things around your house, how to repair your own vehicles, and how to use these skills to generate an income.
- **Hunting and fishing.** A critical part of your long-term survival strategy should be learning how to obtain food without relying on a grocery store. Skills like hunting and fishing are both things you should be learning how to do now, before things get bad.
- **Gardening and canning.** When it comes down to being able to feed your family, there's no better way to ensure your ability to put food on the table than growing it yourself. One of the most important skills you can have is being able to grow and preserve your own food.

INVEST IN LAND

When looking at long-term strategies to ensure your financial future, having your own land is something that ranks right up there at the top of the list. If you're in the financial position to do so, start looking at where you ultimately want to end up. Here are some considerations that you need to keep in mind.

Water Sources

From freshwater springs and rivers to underground well water, having a clean and renewable water source is one of the most important factors to look at when purchasing land.

- What water sources are on the land?
- Are they renewable and will they be there year-round?
- Is the property graded in a way that allows for the creation of a pond or cistern to catch rainwater?

Population Density

The farther away you are from large areas of people, the safer you'll be during a collapse scenario. During an economic collapse, areas with the highest population densities will be most vulnerable to high levels of social unrest and crime. These areas will experience the highest likelihood for epidemics and disease and will see the highest death tolls due to lack of resources and sanitation.

Self-Sufficiency

Look for land with the ability to sustain your lifestyle. This could include having enough sunlight to support the use of solar panels for energy to finding a location that provides adequate resources to feed your family.

Natural Resources

- How easy is it to grow food on your land?
- Does the area support a population of wild animals for hunting?
- Can you easily raise livestock on the land?

(34) Surviving a Job Loss

The loss of a job can be just as traumatizing as any of the other disasters and emergency scenarios discussed in this book. It's also one of the most likely scenarios we'll discuss, which is why everyone needs to be prepared to face this possibility.

HOW TO PREPARE FOR A LOSS OF EMPLOYMENT
Start an Emergency Fund

If you skipped over the section on building your emergency fund, please go back and read that section. Having an emergency fund is the only way you can ensure you'll have the money to survive an extended period of unemployment.

In the past, most experts recommended having about a month's worth of income in your emergency fund; because of today's volatile job market that number should probably be a lot higher. A more realistic number, based on the time it takes to find a job in today's marketplace, is probably closer to six to nine months.

Build Your Stockpiles

The last thing you ever want to worry about is being able to feed your family during a time of unemployment. Losing your income is stressful enough; not being able to feed a hungry child is beyond anything I care to think about.

To ensure you and your family never go hungry, start building your emergency food pantry now. Having even a couple of months' worth of food on hand means your grocery bill is one less expense you'll have to worry about while you don't have a regular income. You'll be able to focus your full attention on finding a new job or starting a new business.

Build Your Network

One of the first steps in surviving a job loss is getting back to work as soon as possible. That means being proactive and preparing for the possibility of losing your job now.

The more people you have in your corner, the better your chances are of finding employment. That means you need to start networking. From social networking sites like LinkedIn to attending industry trade shows and mixers, you need to get out there and meet people who can help you further your career. People are much more likely to hire someone they know than some guy whose only way of finding a job is blasting out thousands of resumes.

Start Supplementing Your Income

Now is the time to start figuring out alternative sources of income.

- Do you have things you can sell online?
- Do you have a talent you can turn into a side business?
- Does your current job present opportunities to engage clients on the side?

Grab a pad of paper and start listing all of the ways you can start bringing in some extra cash. Not only will this help you increase your emergency fund, but you'll have a list of things to immediately fall back on should you lose your job without warning.

Rethink Your Budget

If you're facing a pending job loss, you need to take another serious look at your budget. Your main concern is shelter, food and water, and keeping the lights on. Anything beyond those needs should be put on hold or paid only when the essentials are taken care of. If you're working on getting out of debt, that may have to take a backseat for a while until you regain your stability.

(35) Surviving a Recession and Total Economic Collapse

If you weren't directly affected by the last recession, there's a good chance you probably know a number of people who were. During the 2008 economic crisis, millions of hardworking Americans suddenly found themselves in some major financial trouble. Unfortunately, many people in the United States have already forgotten how bad things were and have returned to their reckless spending and debt-loving ways. But there's one thing we can all be sure of, and that is, at the very least, another recession is coming. It's really unavoidable. If you study history, somewhere around every ten years America faces a recession. With this in mind, doesn't it make sense to prepare for something we can predict is coming?

RECESSION-PROOF YOUR INCOME

One thing you must prepare for in light of a recession is a loss of income. During the recession of 2008, millions of unprepared people suddenly found themselves out of work. While many were eligible for unemployment, the benefits were usually only a fraction of what they made at their jobs.

To truly be prepared, start finding alternative sources of income. This can be anything from starting a side business to selling things online on sites like eBay. The important thing really isn't what you're doing; it's having something you can fall back on should you unexpectedly lose your job.

PAY OFF YOUR DEBT

During the last recession, many people lost their property because they took on massive amounts of debt. When economic problems hit, the banks and your creditors are going to be going into overdrive trying to collect on overdue accounts. The last thing you need to worry about during a recession is losing your home or your property because you never really owned it to begin with. Now is the time to start paying down your debt and becoming the master of your money rather than a slave to it.

STAY LIQUID AND ALWAYS HAVE CASH ON HAND

When preparing for a recession, always have cash that's instantly accessible during a crisis. Your emergency fund is useless if you don't have access to it. When planning for a rainy day, separate your funds. During the 2008 recession people saw their stocks dive, their 401(k) accounts disappear, and many found themselves unable to access their capital that they so badly needed. Your emergency fund should never be looked at as a money-making investment, but instead as an insurance account that is there to protect you and your family from financial ruin.

DON'T COUNT ON THE GOVERNMENT

The government is tapped out! From bank bailouts to extended unemployment benefits, the government spent billions upon billions of taxpayer dollars trying to prevent the total collapse of the system. While there's debate about whether or not any of that money actually helped the situation (in my opinion it only postponed the inevitable), the fact is the country is broke, and there simply isn't enough money in the world to bail us out the next time things go bad.

PREPARE TO THRIVE

During times of economic recession, there are always those who end up profiting from the chaos. While I don't advise taking advantage of people, I do advise putting yourself in a position where you can at least take advantage of the situation. During the last crisis, thousands of stores across the country went bankrupt. During this process many were forced to sell off or liquidate their merchandise at a fraction of the cost. Those who weren't burdened with debt were able to pick up essential supplies at deeply discounted prices. The same was true with housing and land. When the market is depressed, people who have money can get good deals. Your preparedness may pay off in ways you didn't expect.

HOW TO SURVIVE A TOTAL ECONOMIC COLLAPSE

All hell is going to break loose when people wake up one morning and realize their money's gone. Think it can't happen? Think again!

History is filled with examples of countries that have failed due to economic problems. In 1998, Argentina's economic crisis plunged the country into chaos causing widespread unemployment, riots, and the eventual fall of the government. The downfall of the Soviet Union in the late 1980s brought major food shortages, food rationing, and violent uprisings to the region.

Are We Heading Towards an Economic Collapse?

I believe we are witnessing the slow painful downfall of the economy of the United States and many other areas of the world. While I believe the problems that started this mess go back quite some time, I think the banking crisis of 2008 really started to push the economy to the point of no return.

Twenty years ago, most people would have said you were crazy for thinking the U.S. financial system could collapse. Even today, most of the U.S. is either unaware or has forgotten how closely we came to a complete collapse of the financial system during the banking crisis of 2008. I've personally talked to major Wall Street investors who were literally hiding money under their mattresses because they believed the system was about to collapse.

Six years after the crisis that threatened to plunge the entire world into another Great Depression, very little has actually changed; in fact, I would argue things have gotten much worse.

At the time of this writing:

- The United States is over $17 trillion in debt, with unfunded liabilities that make the actual debt number somewhere around $120 trillion.
- Since 2001, the U.S. has lost 5.1 million manufacturing jobs, all but destroying what was once the largest and most robust manufacturing base in the world.

- The federal government is borrowing unprecedented amounts of money, to the tune of almost $1 trillion a year.

No matter how the government or the media tries to spin the numbers, the reality is there's really no way out of the situation. In my opinion, we are looking at one of the biggest Ponzi schemes of all time. I believe the only reason the whole system hasn't collapsed is because of the $17 trillion in debt the U.S. government has racked up. If it wasn't for the debt, combined with the Federal Reserve that's been running the printing presses 24/7, this country would look a whole lot different.

From bank bailouts and corporate welfare to a never-ending supply of unemployment checks and government assistance, this country only looks healthy because the government is doing everything it can to maintain the scam. Instead of the bread lines of the 1920s, we now have 47 million people on food stamps and half the country counting on at least one government program to pay their bills.

The real numbers that nobody wants to talk about seem to indicate the United States and the rest of the world are heading towards some major economic troubles—I believe a complete meltdown of the financial system.

A second possible cause is something called a black swan event, which basically is an unprecedented and unexpected event that can have devastating consequences. In the case of the U.S. economy, it could be something like a large-scale terror attack or possibly a cyberattack aimed at the financial markets that push our already struggling economy over the edge.

This second scenario should be most worrisome for those who haven't started preparing because if it happens, you're going to be in for some major trouble.

What to Expect Following an Economic Collapse

In my opinion, today's world is not set up to survive a full-scale economic collapse. Most people still stubbornly refuse to believe the reality of the situation and continue to spend like there's no tomorrow. I hate to say it, but today's world is anything but stable, and during a full-scale economic collapse we're going to see some major problems.

Inability to access money. Once the system goes, your electronic money is going with it. Access to your credit cards, ATMs and pretty much any form of electronic payment will probably be suspended almost immediately.

A rush for paper currency. While I do believe paper currency will quickly become useless, in the immediate aftermath of the collapse, people are going to be doing anything they can to get their hands on it. In their minds it will still have a perceived value, and without access to their bank accounts, people are going to be in full-blown panic mode.

This makes it extremely important to always have paper currency on hand. In the days and weeks after collapse, whatever cash you have can be used to buy any last minute-supplies you might need to survive the crisis.

Supply chain backups and stoppages. During a full-scale collapse it's likely that nationwide delivery systems will stop. Once that happens, it's going to be almost impossible to find food and any other supplies that you've grown accustomed to finding in your local grocery store. The average store simply doesn't have enough food on hand to last more than a couple of days. Once those supplies dry up, they won't be restocked.

Chaos on the streets. Even on a good day, people can be unpredictable. Add in an economy that's collapsed and people scrambling to figure out how they're going to feed their families, and I'm pretty sure you'll be able to get a good idea of what things are going to look like.

One of the largest threats you will face during a collapse is going to be people who failed to prepare. These people are going to be desperate, and once they run out of the small amount of food they have at home, they're going to come looking for yours.

Criminals targeting everyone. Criminals will be doing everything they can to take advantage of the chaos that ensues after an economic collapse. These people will prey on everyone, especially those who look like easy targets, and will more than likely thrive during the aftermath.

Terror attacks. When things go bad, there will likely be a large number of groups trying to land the final blow. Rogue governments, terrorist organizations and lone psychopaths will all be looking to use the situation to push their agenda.

Surviving an Economic Collapse

While there's very little we can do to prevent the world from plunging itself off the financial cliff, there are a number of things you can do on a personal level. The best way to survive a full economic collapse is to

- understand that the threat is real.
- follow the principles outlined throughout the book, including doing your own threat assessment and SWOT analysis based on the threat (chapter one).
- develop a plan for long-term financial security (outlined in chapter thirty-three).
- start living a more self-reliant lifestyle.

In my opinion, the writing's on the wall; there's no way this doesn't end badly. You can choose to believe media pundits and government officials who have a vested interest in artificially pumping up a failing economy, or you can learn from the lessons of the past and prepare for what's coming.

Remember, the key to surving any type of disaster is doing your own research, identifying the most likely threats, and then doing everything you can to prepare for those threats. The choice of what you do with the information provided in this book is yours, but at the very least, consider the threats that are outlined and then figure out how you would respond to those threats in a way that ensures your surival.

ABOUT THE AUTHOR

Robert Richardson, founder and the writer at offgridsurvival .com, one of the top emergency preparedness/survival websites in the world, is a preparedness and survival training expert with over 20 years of real-world experience.

His articles and advice on preparedness issues have been featured by numerous national and international media outlets, including the Huffington Post, ABC News, CNN, Yahoo News and some of the top outdoor/ preparedness related websites in the world. His broad range of experience and wealth of knowledge makes him one of the most sought-after survival experts, with his advice appearing on hundreds of industry websites and publications.

With decades of experience in both wilderness and urban survival issues, he uses his real-world insights to help train and educate people in a way that most so-called survival experts can only theorize about.

When he's not teaching or writing about preparedness topics, he spends a lot of his time hunting and fishing in some of the most remote wilderness areas of the world. He writes about his outdoor adventures at monsterfishandgame.com.

For more information on preparedness and survival training, or to contact Robert visit www.offgridsurvival.com

ACKNOWLEDGEMENTS

I would like to thank The Lord for his mercy, for blessing me with countless opportunities, and giving me the ability to write about these topics and hopefully do my small part to help people in this world.

I would like to thank my awesome wife, Jennifer, and our three wonderful children for giving me the inspiration and motivation to write this book. Without them and their love I would be lost.

Thank you to all the readers at offgridsurvival.com, and thank you to those who purchased this book.

Other fine Living Ready books are available from your local bookstore and online suppliers. Visit our website at www.livingreadyonline.com. Living Ready® is a registered trademark of F+W Media.

18   17   16   15   14   5   4   3   2   1

ISBN 978-1-4403-3677-5

Distributed in the U.K. and Europe by F&W Media International, LTD
Brunel House, Forde Close, Newton Abbot, TQ12 4PU, UK
Tel: (+44) 1626 323200, Fax: (+44) 1626 323319, E-mail: enquiries@fwmedia.com

Distributed in Canada by Fraser Direct
100 Armstrong Avenue, Georgetown, Ontario, Canada L7G 5S4
Tel: (905) 877-4411

Distributed in Australia by Capricorn Link, P.O. Box 704, S. Windsor NSW, 2756 Australia
Tel: (02) 4560-1600, Fax: (02) 4577-5288, E-mail: books@capricornlink.com.au

Edited by Jacqueline Musser and Kelsea Daulton
Cover design by Clare Finney
Production coordinated by Debbie Thomas

BUG OUT BAG INVENTORY REVIEW SHEET

This five-page Bug Out Bag inventory Review Sheet will make packing and reviewing your Bug Out Bag's contents efficient and foolproof. Download it for free at **livingready online.com/bug-out-bag-packing-list**

MORE BOOKS ON SURVIVAL AND PREPAREDNESS

Build the Perfect Bug Out Bag: Your 72-Hour Disaster Survival Kit by Creek Stewart

Living Ready Pocket Manual First Aid by James Hubbard, The Survival Doctor™

Food Storage for Self-Sufficiency and Survival by Angela Paskett

AVAILABLE ONLINE AND IN BOOKSTORES EVERYWHERE!

Get free survival and preparedness tips! Join our mailing list at livingreadyonline.com.

Become a fan of our Facebook page: facebook.com/LivingReady